MTV | UNCENSORED

Edited by Jacob Hoye
Compiled by David P. Levin and Stuart Cohn
Photo Editor: Walter Einenkel

POCKET BOOKS

New York London Toronto Sydney Singapore

An Original Publication of MTV Books/Pocket Books

POCKET BOOKS, a division of Simon & Schuster, Inc.
1230 Avenue of the Americas, New York, NY 10020

ISBN: 0-7434-2682-7

First MTV Books/Pocket Books hardcover printing
August 2001

10 9 8 7 6 5 4 3 2 1

POCKET and colophon are registered trademarks of
Simon & Schuster, Inc.

Printed in the U.S.A.

editor: Jacob Hoye · additional editing: Liz Brooks ·
editorial direction: Dave Sirulnick
photo editor: Walter Einenkel

design direction: Jeffrey Keyton · art direction:
Christopher Truch · book design and page layout:
Laura Lindgren and Celia Fuller / Lindgren/Fuller
Design with Jacob Hoye and Walter Einenkel

talent and staff voices compiled by David P. Levin and
Stuart Cohn · artist voices compiled by Liz Brooks,
Walter Einenkel, and Jacob Hoye

from interviews conducted by Mark Doctorow, Peter
Menzies, Jennifer Demme, Peter Slack, Ira Fields,
Adam Abernathy, Carissa Potenza, Matthew
Anderson, Andrea Duncan, Abbie Kearse, Natalie
Rotman, Shannon Marek, Heather Parry, Liane Su,
Danielle Weiss, Eric Stringer, Beth Turerack, Carlo
Ocando, Cheryl Horner, C. Scott Gorman, Chris
Connelly, William Maclachlan, Natalia Garcia, David
Higby, Eva Neu, Nandi Pointer, Chris Martello, Ryan
Pender, John Norris, Sari Siegel, Pete Wilkinson,
Stuart Cohn, and David P. Levin

rights and clearances: Andrea LaBate Glanz, Michelle
Gurney, and Lori Allred · legal: Robin Silverman

special contributors: Kurt Loder, Chris Connelly,
Britney Spears, Nelly, Denis Leary, Tom Delonge,
David Silveria, Tabitha Soren, and Al Yankovic

all the good boys and girls · each and every one of us · those we left behind · one and all · the little girl that lives down the lane · the Gipper · the birds · all the tea in China · every time I ever heard
t · the time being · a better view · all the world · starters · free · the love of God · a few dollars more · crying out loud · real · your information · keeps · better or worse · example · your own good · the bes
breath · shame · no reason at all · a good time call · a change of pace · a song · forty days and forty nights · spotless dishes · years to come · something new · a little more · Lucas Beckett · a day · art's sak
ess dishes · something out of the ordinary · score and seven years ago · all other calls · whiter whites · the grave · a change of pace · no reason at all · a spell · healthy teeth and strong bones · instance
night's sleep · a few dollars more · a brief moment · shame · fresh breath · the last time · the most part · a while · ever and a day · the mercy seat is waiting · a limited time only · the times they are a-changi
ur great plans · everlasting peace · sure · a free sample · Rachel · the chains of the sea · a time · the moment · the record · the road · a good little doggie · all it's worth · the love of a good man · your heal
future · good reason · all that · a season · all one knows · good · nothing · form's sake · love alone · the nonce · the boys · the team · all it's worth · Pete's sake · Divine · a loop · keeps · laughs · kicks
rs · Sam · serious · the hell of it · a lark · a goof · the long haul · it · the cuff · honest · ever and a day · the love of Mike · granted · dead · lost · one · you · wear · all that · life · miles and miles · Mr. Goodbar · re
t soldier · Heaven's sake · Jack · the night · the term of your sentence · ladies only · love or money · me and my gal · richer or poorer · the first time · the love of it · the pure thrill of it · whom the bell tol
eyes only · we are weak · your thoughts · sore eyes · a horse · man or beast · my peeps · the moon · trouble · glory · mercy · a bruisin' · the count · tomorrow we may die · Jeremy · directory assistance
nows what tomorrow will bring · all I care · all intents and purposes · every hung-up person in the whole wide universe · all practical purposes · all the world · all you're worth · days on end · goo
ure · goodness sake · hours at a time · Lindsay · days at a time · hours on end · kicks and giggles · old time's sake · peanuts · pity's sake · sale · short · that matter · the asking · the best · the better · th
of it · the heck of it · the life of me · the love of a good woman · what it's worth · your dining pleasure · your convenience · your own part · your own sake · good behavior · the ride · broke · Leigh · the gusto
roat · the hat · the jugular · the mill · the hills · all I know · the last roundup · attendance · a steward · dear life · leather · Chloe · ice cream · a penny · a pound · joy · eternity · life everlasting · a needle in
ack · bear · the silver lining · number one · each other · lost time · more than I bargained · the record books · the course · your supper · service · a flight attendant · the memories · the good times · the grad
I go I · tat · your britches · Alex · grabs · the other shoe to drop · the goose · the gander · all the gold in Fort Knox · hire · sale by owner · the duration · want of a nail · your own protection · a good fit · you
a letter · a telegram · a check that's in the mail · your free gift · a lift · the love of the game · Esme, with love and squalor · a sec · life · Zelda · 20 years · children thirteen and over · adults only · good weathe
nny day · rain · another look · lease · more information · no money down · lease payment · payment options · healthy teeth and strong gums · your at-home enjoyment · Arabella · liberty and justice for al
a free catalog · your friend · love in all the wrong places · those though inclined · Deonnie · a hug and a kiss · a whole lot more · your shopping needs · your homecare needs · all your laundry needs · freshe
· a hunk of cheese · a rainy day · your homework tonight · a bit of fun · a little fun · best taste · a sign · a place to call our own · Anya · a place to hang your hat · a closer, cleaner shave · charity · the hills
ncher · a better tomorrow · a smoke · a phone call · gas, food & lodging · the term of your natural life · world peace · the children · children of all races · a dream · Destiny · I've come from Alabama with
on my knee · truth, justice and the American way · the elderly and handicapped · pennies · pennies less · a place in the sun · a few minutes · a minute · five minutes · hours · months on end · years ar
ever and ever · ever after · a walk · a stroll · a dance · a walk in the park · Anna Maeve · a walk in the woods · a long walk · a swim · a dip · deposit/payment · withdrawal · last five transactions · accou
ces · fast relief · temporary relief · a farce · a movie · a flick · your country · eternity · our top story · your local listings · arrivals · Nevada · departures · everyone in the class · all good men to come to the a
r country · something · the answer · the correct answer · the time of your life · a bathroom · a break · a coffee break · a short break · lunch, babe · profit · gain · Thalia · something out of the ordinary
thing new · those who dare · room service · the timid · the meek shall inherit the earth · the faint of heart · a romp in the park · nothing and your chicks for free · the cheap seats · intelligent life in the univers
ng · bad breath · your retirement · Shane · your financial planning · your financial future · a bus · the train · my man · the right moment · my lady · someone to meet me · something positive · Lucas · the rig
your collection · the ride of your life · your listening pleasure · the next available representative · the lonely · ever more · tomorrow may never come · forgiveness · a good woman is above rubies ·
urger today · he's a jolly good fellow · it ain't nobody's business but my own · the weary and downtrodden · me and my monkey · a friend of mine · the afterglow · Griffin · spacious skies · long-term relationsh
mmer sublet · the way out · the perfect getaway · the perfect holiday meal · my other shoe · a minute there · art thou, Romeo · a small fee · the very first time · the girl next door · the kid in you · Caitlin · th
ries · those hard to reach places · all the fellas · the summer · told · a balanced diet · today's specials · the ladies in the house · club members only · UV protection · 84 Henry Street · ever young

Photography Credits

This Is Not Propaganda

This book would not have been possible if not for the dedication, faith, kindness, patience, and tolerance of the many astonishingly cool people who follow. We'd need another book to fully detail our debt to them. Hopefully, these humble shout-outs will suffice.

Super thanks to: Lisa Silfen, who offered the opportunity, nurtured, mentored, and directed us from there to here · Dave Sirulnick, for guiding us through the forest · Donald Silvey, for his unflagging support and encouragement · Jeffrey Keyton, for opening our eyes · Van Toffler, for turning it in the right direction · Laura Lindgren and Celia Fuller, for indulging us · Kara Welsh, for taking the ride · Donna O'Neill, for being on our side · Lori Feldman and Liz Rosenberg, for trying · Wenonah and Lucas Hoye, for waiting. · John Reed, for... · Kurt Loder and Chris Connelly, for playing along · Andrea LaBate Glanz and Michelle Gurney, for enduring many insane and last-minute requests · Tom Freston and Judy McGrath, for making it all possible.

Also thanks to those whose efforts, kindness, or company made our lives a hell of a lot lovelier: Alex Coletti · Allison Klein · Anastasia Hays · Angela Castro · Anthony Jacobs · Audra Cowf · Avery Coburn · Beverlee, Richard and Abby Brooks · Bill Flanagan · Billy Sanford · Bob Dylan · Brian Blatz · Brigitte Smith · Carissa Potenza · Carole Robinson · Carson Daly · Chip Butterman · Chris Green · Chris McGhee · Christina Dugger · Christina Norman · Christine Alloro · Christopher Truch · Dan Dimtro · Daniel Bobker · Dave Pfeffer · David Moscow · David Saslow · Deb Savo · Deborah Gibson · Deklah Polansky · Ed Paparo · Elli Cola · Eric Wybenga · Erika Laden · Ernest Boyd · Evans Ward · Fran Gullo · Frank Micelotta · Geoffrey Kloske · Geremy Jasper · Greer Kessel Hendricks · Heidi Eskenazi · Hillary Cohen · Incorrect Music · J.J. Jackson · Jade Hoye · Jamie Sandin · Janet Rolle · Jay Levey · Jeanette Petersson · Jeff Kravitz · Jen Demme · Jen Mandel · Jeri Rose · Jesse Ignjatovic · Jewel · Ji Yoo · Jim DeBarros · Joe Schram · Joellen Charlot-Duffy · John Eaton · John Norris · John Piccirillo · Jon Murray · Kate Raudenbush · Kate Sawall · Kathleen Voege · Kathryn Hansen · Kathy Flynn · Kelly Alferi · Ken Freda · Kurt Williamson · Laura Murphy · Liate Stehlik · Linda Dingler · Lisa Feuer · Lori Allred · Marcela Romero · Mark Doctorow · Marnie Malter · Marshall Eisen · Melanie Gomez · Michael Rapaport · Michelle Dorn · Michelle Mulligan · Mitch Kornfeld · Myra Correa · Nan Tozzi · Natalie Rotman · Nick Cave · Nina Diaz · Nina Goodman · Patricia Connelly · Paul Melcher · Paula DeSaro · Pauly Shore · Penelope Haynes · Peter Dougherty · Preston Kevin Lewis · Q · Raffaela Saccone · Ralph and Josephine Corso · Raquel Bruno · Reggie Bradford · Richard and Valerie Hoye · Rikki Ades · Rob Dixter · Robert, Francie, Herbert, Nick and Timothy Einenkel · Robert Imbriani · Robin Silverman · Rockpants.com · Roger Coletti · Ryan Ingrasin · Samantha Amell · Sandra Meadows · Sarah James · Sarah Lazin · Sari Siegel · Sasha Wolff · Scott Friedman · Shannon Knapp · Stephen C. Ng · Steve Denson · Suzanne O'Neill · Tessa Beck · Tommy Cody · Twisne Fan · Wendy Gaswirth

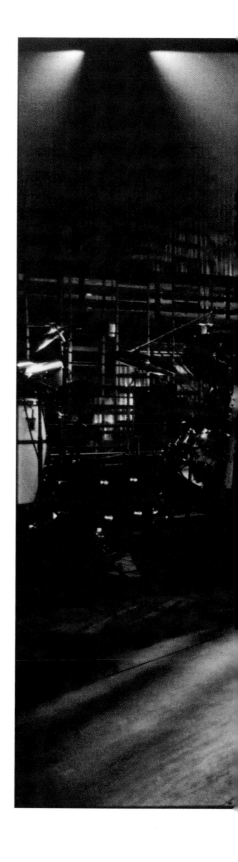

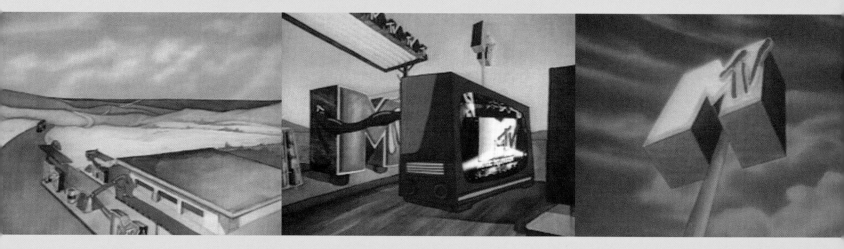

Interview with the M

MTV NEWS Okay, we're ready for M.

M'S PUBLICIST Great. We're expecting M any minute. Can I see what your shot looks like?

[*Forty-five minutes pass*]

MTV NEWS So where's M?

M'S PUBLICIST Hung up in traffic. Should be here any minute.

MTV NEWS We have an hour, right?

M'S PUBLICIST Absolutely. Can I check your shot? [*looks at monitor*] We need softer light.

[*Thirty-five minutes pass*]

M'S PUBLICIST Let me see the shot again. [*looks, frowns*] Can't you make it any softer?

[*Ten minutes pass*]

MTV INTERN M's here!

[*M enters, surrounded by five people, and heads into makeup.*]

[*Twenty minutes pass*]

M [*off-camera*] I *hate* this outfit! It makes me humongous! I look like the Gateway Arch!

[*Ten minutes pass*]

M'S PUBLICIST You know about M's charity work, right? And you know he's got his own record label, clothing line, and website?

MTV NEWS Right.

M'S PUBLICIST I just want to make sure you're not going to dwell on that whole who-made-you thing, because that is just so *played* by now.

MTV NEWS Well, I . . .

M'S PUBLICIST M doesn't want to talk about it.

MTV NEWS But it's part of the public record. Can't M at least address the question of—

M'S PUBLICIST *No.* I am telling you that if you try to ask, M will get up and walk out. M has always had a good relationship with you. I cannot understand why you would want to—

M [*Sweeping in, sitting down*] Okay, okay! Sorry to keep you waiting. Can I see the shot? [*looks at monitor*] How's my hair?

M'S HAIR PERSON It just needs a little fuss. That light is really harsh.

M'S PUBLICIST You know what? Can we shoot M from the other side? [*sotto voce to producer*] M's a little sensitive about the "TV" tattoo.

[*Five minutes pass*]

MTV NEWS Well, M, it's been quite a year for you. How are you holding up?

M It's been crazy; I mean . . . [*checks pager*] Hang on a moment, Dre's hitting me on the two-way.

[*Three minutes pass*]

MTV NEWS So, M, it's been twenty years now . . .

M And it still feels like yesterday, when I was just another sans serif on a draftsperson's table. I've seen so many of my letter-buddies fade away since, you know: A&M, RCA, J.J. . . . you know, people today don't even talk about E.T. like they used to! So just to still be around is a pretty big achievement. I owe so much to the people I broke in with: Martha and Mark and Nina and that blonde guy—what was his name?

MTV NEWS Uh, Alan. [*gingerly*] The twentieth anniversary must certainly get you thinking about those early days, huh?

M You are so right. It was tough, I admit. First, not knowing who your real creators are . . . Fred Seibert? Patti Rogoff? Some graphic arts major from Manhattan Design Studios? Someone said I was pulled out of the garbage—but I'm sorry, I can*not* deal with that. Secretly, I think I always hoped it was David Felton or Gail Sparrow. But everyone wanted credit, and frankly, I still don't know for sure.

MTV NEWS M, did you ever see your father cry?

M What the hell are you talking about?

MTV NEWS Never mind. You were saying . . .

M I still remember all the acclaim . . . the moon man, the flag, "I want my" you-know-what . . . It got so I couldn't leave the house without some vowel wanting to "blend" with me . . . and then—[*pause. Eyes well up.*]

MTV NEWS [*hands M a tissue*] Diceman going postal at the Video Music Awards—that must have really hurt.

M Andrew Dice Clay? Who cared about him? But never in a million years did I think Bob Pittman would just . . . *leave!* For NBC, okay, but for . . . Century 21! Oh, God . . . [*starts to sob*] Dumped for . . . for . . . *real estate!* The *humiliation!* [*silence*] Then came that . . . that . . . *game* show . . .

MTV NEWS You mean *Remote Control*, MTV's first hit series that wasn't really based on mus—

M Sure, sure, I got a little difficult then. Partied a little too hard, got a little thick around the bottom. You try going out in public and having the same thing yelled at you over and over: "Hey, I thought the M in MTV stood for 'Music'! I guess it stands for 'Money'!" Stands for *money*!

MTV NEWS That must have hurt.

M Didn't they know about those years when I had to *beg* to get on a cable system? Or all those bands that didn't stand a *chance* on FM radio without my love and support? [*tears up*] My boys T and V, they tried to get me into rehab but . . . I guess I wasn't listening. I still remember getting drunk with the E in ESPN—now there's a letter with some *serious* self-esteem issues.

MTV NEWS So what pulled you out?

M [*smiles*] Well, I'd get a lot of big love at our events . . . like the VMAs and the Movie Awards. Janet was always so supportive in troubled times. But come on, who do you think?

MTV NEWS [*understanding*] Ah . . .

M You see? Madonna made me understand that after the Jesus Joneses and Another Bad Creations and *Trashed*s and *You Wrote It, You Watch It*s and *Mouth to Mouth*s—we'd always have each other, you know what I'm saying? I mean, when this person stands by you, with her love and creativity, what else do you need? I mean, aside from a really kick-ass ad sales department! [*embarrassed*] Excuse my language. Can I say "ad sales department" on MTV?

MTV NEWS Not to pry into your personal life, but you've had quite a few intimate relationships over the years.

M So true, so true, starting in the early '80s with that bad boy Rod—I was his first non-blonde!—and ending up with that good girl Mandy—I was her first love, period! And when we started going international [*throaty chuckle*] well, I could tell you some stories—but you know what? What happens overseas stays overseas. At least until I turn forty! [*laughs*] Boxers or briefs, baby!

MTV NEWS You and Michael Jackson really kept the gossip columns filled back in the day.

M Oh, that was special. [*blushing*] We shared years of happiness. For a while I thought it would never end. But when that "King of Pop" deal started, I sort of knew it was over.

MTV NEWS Tell us—who were your favorites?

M Well, let's see: I never could resist Snoop . . . and God, I loved Eddie, even if it was so hard for him to love me back . . . and Stipe, before he got pretentious . . . [*to self*] It's like he doesn't even *know* me now. Sad.

Zack's the same way. Mariah took me places I *never* thought I'd go. Courtney? God, was she fun. Still is, come to think of it. I gotta look for her online sometime. Prince was terrific, but . . .

MTV NEWS Yes?

M Let's just say you shouldn't be learning how to say "hello" when it's time to say "goodbye." Other guys don't realize when the magic is gone and it's time to move on. David Lee Roth, I mean you!

MTV NEWS Any secret passions?

M People don't always remember how intense it got with Paula. [*low sultry chuckle*] Ah, maybe that's a good thing. I still wish it hadn't ended with her like it did. I really thought it was going to work out with those Prodigy boys—I do love to dance, you know. Hey, everyone knew about me and L.L., right?

MTV NEWS Yes, they did.

M Good. Seemed Chuck D was always there for me. And while everyone remembers me and Cyndi, it's been just as wonderful with Gwen. She's a doll. So thoughtful. But you know who was my absolute favorite? Bono. What a person, onstage and off. Not that you could always tell the difference! [*laughs*]

MTV NEWS What was it like being so tight with Axl?

M [*exhales*] Talk about having problems with commitment! Never a dull moment, I'll tell you that. I'm so glad he's coming back. I've really missed him . . . and, of course, I miss the ones who aren't coming back: Tupac, Kurt, Biggie, Michael Hutchence . . . I wish they were here right now.

M'S PUBLICIST You do realize M needs to be out of here no later than 5:15.

MTV NEWS But you promised us we'd have an hour!

M'S PUBLICIST He has a flight to catch.

MTV NEWS I just have a few one-sheet questions. M, what's in your DVD player right now?

M'S PUBLICIST M's leaving now!

MTV NEWS Just one more question: M, any regrets?

M Oh, you know what I say? "Mistakes, many; regrets, none!"

MTV NEWS That's a great philosophy.

M It really is. Of course, it doesn't explain Ugly Kid Joe, but what does? Bye, everyone!

PAPARAZZI [*off-camera*] M! M! M! Over here, M! M, please!

Chris Connelly

Video Music Awards

STEVEN TYLER It's like a good/bad dream where you're walking around meeting all these people and you're like, "Wow, I can't believe this is really happening." And then you go out in front of the cameras and read your little bit off the thing, get your award, walk offstage, and hand it back to someone. That's the music business right there. "Here it is, give it back." Then you get raked across the coals of hell in the press tent. From one insane moment to another.

JOHN SYKES, former executive The VMA's idea came from Bob Pittman wanting to do a signature channel event. We got Don Ohlmeyer, an accomplished sports producer, to do the show for us instead of the traditional Oscars® group. By that time MTV was doing fairly well, so we were able to book some pretty substantial artists. Rod Stewart, Tina Turner, and Madonna. It redefined music events on television by trying to relay our sarcastic tone to the big TV event.

DOUG HERZOG, former executive I think if you look at the show from 1984 to now, it's a great indication of how MTV has evolved, and you can trace the history through the presenters and the performers and so on.

KURT LODER Things happen that will never happen at the Academy Awards® or the Emmys®. MTV is just great at staging shows like this. There's a whole department of people at MTV who just specialize in parties and fun. I think this is one of the few organizations that has that.

MOBY One of the nice things about the Video Music Awards is the parties. It's fun if you find yourself in a hotel suite at seven o'clock in the morning and there are rock stars and models and movie stars and they're all drunk and making out with each other.

BOB PITTMAN, MTV co-founder The hope was that it would become an annuity. That it would become *the* thing, we would make it into the hot party, the show that the artists really cared about and viewers would look forward to. You know, "If there's one show I'm gonna watch a year it's that one." Because it sort of captures what's been happening in music for the year. And it's lived up to its promise.

ROB THOMAS Most of the people I'm fortunate enough to meet I would have given anything to get a ticket to one of their shows just a couple years ago. When I think about the fact that I can go there and meet people like Eric Clapton and Sting, that amazes me.

You press
the button,
BING,
all the stars
go whoom,
and there
you are in
the middle
of it.

—JIMMY THE CAB DRIVER

VMA 1999

TOMMY LEE Awesome! Best one I've been to.

SALLI FRATTINI, production executive I remember our first meeting at the Met where we had representatives from all the theaters in a room. And the average age was of course above the average age of the MTV viewers—or workers, for that matter. And after we did a whole presentation, one of the gentlemen, who had glasses down here on his nose, little bifocals, looked up and he said, "Is this one of those events people smoke pot at?"

LENNY KRAVITZ It was a mix of the classic world and the rock 'n' roll world.

VAN TOFFLER, president, MTV and MTV 2 Chris had only rehearsed two jokes. One of them was, "I'm the first black man on the stage of the Met without a mop," at which point I was accosted by all the Met people about how he couldn't do that. I promptly told them, "I don't control Chris Rock."

BRITNEY SPEARS I was really nervous. All those celebrities watching me. I was really freaking out.

KID ROCK I could barely get out of my house for two weeks, my head was so big.

BRIAN GRADEN, president, programming and production About a half-hour before the show, I'm doing that nervous pacing thing because at that point the show's in God's hands. No matter how much planning you've done, no matter how good or bad your dress rehearsal was, the show is live. And at eight P.M. the show is going to start and Chris Rock is going to come onto the stage and is going to say whatever he's going to say. And in fact, he wasn't afraid to offend absolutely everyone. So by that point I said, "I'm no longer nervous because the show is great, but I better start drinking now because after the show we're going to hear it from everybody." Luckily everybody was a pretty good sport. Ricky Martin and others kind of played along. But he spared no one.

DATE September 9
LOCATION Metropolitan Opera House, New York
HOST Chris Rock

PERFORMERS

Kid Rock featuring Run-D.M.C. and Aerosmith	"King of Rock/"Bawitdaba"/ "Walk This Way"
Lauryn Hill	"Lost Ones"/ "Everything Is Everything"
Backstreet Boys	"I Want It That Way/Larger than Life"
Ricky Martin	"She's All I Ever Had"/ "Livin' La Vida Loca"
Nine Inch Nails	"Fragile"
TLC	"No Scrubs"
Fatboy Slim and the Torrance Community Dance Group	"Praise You"
Jay-Z featuring Amil	"Can I Get a . . ." / "Hard Knock Life"/ Jigga"
Britney Spears with *NSYNC	"Baby One More Time"/ "Tearin' Up My Heart"
Eminem featuring Dr. Dre and Snoop Dogg	"My Name Is . . ."/ "Guilty Conscience"/ "Nuthin But a G Thang"

WINNERS

Best Video	Lauryn Hill, "Doo Wop (That Thing)"
Best Male Video	Will Smith, "Miami"
Best Female Video	Lauryn Hill, "Doo Wop (That Thing)"
Best Group Video	TLC, "No Scrubs"
Best Rap Video	Jay-Z featuring Ja Rule and Amil, "Can I Get a . . ."
Best Dance Video	Ricky Martin, "Livin' La Vida Loca"
Best Hip-Hop Video	Beastie Boys, "Intergalactic"
Best Rock Video	Korn, "Freak on a Leash"
Best Pop Video	Ricky Martin, "Livin' La Vida Loca"
Best New Artist in a Video	Eminem, "My Name Is . . ."
Best R&B Video	Lauryn Hill, "Doo Wop (That Thing)"
Viewer's Choice Award	Backstreet Boys, "I Want It That Way"
Breakthrough Video	Fatboy Slim, "Praise You"

TODD OLDHAM I thought Lil' Kim looked great. I love anyone that brave and that bold because the reason it was successful on her was because she wore it like she had a pair of jeans on.

JEN DEMME, producer I remember sitting in the truck and seeing the camera that was recording it and, I was like, "Who just got out of the limo in that blue purply sequin thing and oh my God her boob's exposed!"

We were psyched because who knows what crazy stuff is going to come out of that? So comes time for the best hip-hop awards and Diana, Mary J, and Lil' Kim were presenting and they come out and there was a little banter that was scripted and I guess Diana decided to take it upon herself to seize the moment. She went right up to Lil' Kim and started dangling her boob like, "What is this here?"

TODD OLDHAM Watching Diana Ross feel up Lil' Kim is forever burned in my brain. I don't know if that's a good thing but it's burned in my brain.

SALLI FRATTINI It was the first time Madonna ever met Paul. We wanted to do something special for her. They had a great scene backstage where they were in the talent dressing room, sitting on the floor, sharing a bottle of wine together. I wish we had captured that. I don't think we did, it was nice to see Madonna enamored of somebody.

VAN TOFFLER Judy McGrath and I went backstage to meet Paul McCartney and just as we're about to knock on his dressing room door, we realize he's in there alone playing the piano and we looked at each other like, "Oh my God! It's a real Beatle playing the piano. What are we gonna say to him?" It's one of those moments where you revert to being a 15-year-old.

JA RULE That was a special moment in hip-hop, you know? To have Mrs. Wallace and Mrs. Shakur appear, presenting the Best Rap Video, was hot. And for Jay to win it was hot too, cause he knew Big.

EVE Beautiful, that's the best word to describe it. To see those two up there, that was beautiful. It was just, "Wow!" But then it made you think that's a shame. We lost two powerful influences in hip-hop and there's no reason, they should still be here. That's a shame.

JAY Z I was sittin' next to Backstreet Boys. Backstreet then me. I must be doin' something right.

Ronald Reagan is inaugurated as the fortieth president.

The XXII Olympiad begins in Moscow.

After 444 days, Iran releases 52 American hostages.

Attempting to impress actress Jodie Foster, John Hinckley, Jr., fails in assassination attempt on Reagan outside the Washington Hilton.

Maiden flight of the first U.S. space shuttle *Columbia*.

Scientists identify Acquired Immune Deficiency Syndrome (AIDS).

IBM introduces the first "home" or "personal" computer (the PC).

Prince Charles and Lady Diana Spencer marry in St. Paul's Cathedral on July 29.

Sandra Day O'Connor appointed first female U.S. Supreme Court justice.

Egyptian President Anwar Sadat is assassinated by soldiers at a military parade.

Major League Baseball games are suspended from June 12 to August 9 due to a players' strike.

Muhammad Ali retires from boxing. His career record is 56–5.

Academy Award® Winners

Best Picture: *Ordinary People*
Best Actor: Robert De Niro (*Raging Bull*)
Best Actress: Sissy Spacek (*Coal Miner's Daughter*)

Films

Arthur (Steve Gordon)
Gallipoli (Peter Weir)
An Officer and a Gentleman (Taylor Hackford)
On Golden Pond (Mark Rydell)
Raiders of the Lost Ark (Steven Spielberg)
Chariots of Fire (Hugh Hudson)

Deaths

Actress Natalie Wood (b. 1938)
Jamaican reggae musician Bob Marley (b. 1945)
Songwriter Harry Chapin (b. 1942)

Grammy Award® Winners

Album of the Year: *Double Fantasy*, John Lennon and Yoko Ono
Record of the Year: *Bette Davis Eyes*, Kim Carnes
Best New Artist: Sheena Easton

Births

Justin Timberlake of *NSYNC (January 31)
MTV (August 1)
Britney Spears (December 2)

Before

JON STEWART There was one channel, run by the state. And they knew what you were thinking.

There were around nine channels VHF, maybe four UHF. UHF was always like "I'm Uncle Binky. I host the children's weepy hour," all local, colorful programming. Captain Noah, Uncle Floyd. The regular channels were just straight-up soap operas in the morning, soap operas in the afternoon, cartoons in the four o'clock block. Five o'clock news. Game shows. Very similar to now, but nothing else to watch. So we used to go outside. We used to go—what's the word?—*play* outside.

JANEANE GAROFALO I remember my favorite show, *Bosom Buddies* with Tom Hanks and Peter Scolari, and *SCTV*, which was a sketch comedy show. Those were my two favorite shows in '81.

CHRIS CONNELLY *Saturday Night Live* was in a creative hellhole. A lot of their stars had gone off to movies. Belushi, Aykroyd, Gilda Radner, Bill Murray, and Chevy Chase had already left.

JANEANE GAROFALO *Three's Company* was still on. *Happy Days* was milking it way beyond its years. *M*A*S*H* was still on. These shows had really run out of every plot thing, and everybody looked like they were orange Cheez Doodles with pancake makeup.

JON STEWART When TV programmers ran out of shit to put on the air, they called it like it was. They'd go, "You know what we got? Nothing. We'd love to give you another program—we just can't do it." Dooooooooooooooooooooo. Tone.

ALAN HUNTER All television went off at about one in the morning and there was static.

JON STEWART That was it. That was them giving up. That was a white flag. Now people never give up. It's four in the morning: "You want to dehydrate your meat and make it into jerky?" That's what you're throwing on there. Just give up. Dooooooooooooo.

CHRIS CONNELLY In Manhattan, we got cable TV in 1972 for good reception. Nobody imagined what cable TV would turn into, even as late as '81.

JON STEWART Before cable, TV had rabbit ears antennae. You'd try to get your brother to stand there when the game was on. Channel 9 and channel 11 were tougher to get in. 2, 4, and 7 came in real good. But 9 and 11 where the games were on, very tough. You had to have somebody with the rabbit ears doing a little Baryshnikov.

ED LOVER I didn't have cable.

DR. DRE That's the difference between then and now. In 1977, my father said, "Ah, it won't last a year," paying for television. At that time, you got cable to watch fights, honestly.

ED LOVER Wometco Home Theater. WHT.

DR. DRE Trying to explain to somebody: We're gonna pay to watch television. "You out your mind?"

ED LOVER Couldn't pay the gas bill, how you gonna pay for TV?

JON STEWART When cable came in, suddenly TV didn't have fuzz. I remember that as being the biggest difference. I was going, why does everybody look so clear? That's not what TV's supposed to look like. It's supposed to look like everybody is about to get sent off to space.

DAVE SIRULNICK, news and production executive Cable used to mean HBO, and out-of-town TV stations from Boston, or Philadelphia, or Chicago. Repeats of sitcoms. In early '81, CNN came on the scene, and there was news on all the time. Shortly after that I remember ESPN, a lot of rodeos and things—they didn't have any of those Major League Baseball contracts.

JOHN SYKES, former executive You couldn't see cool music on TV. All we had in those days was *The Midnight Special*, which was a bunch of old guys producing rock 'n' roll on TV. The bands would look into the camera, and the shots were silly and you'd get a combination of Helen Reddy next to the Rolling Stones.

CHRIS CONNELLY Music on TV was in a ghetto. You were so grateful when Elvis Costello turned up on Tom Snyder's show or when the Clash would play *Saturday Night Live*. So many bands hadn't broken through in any major way. The new wave bands, from the Cars or Cheap Trick, to Elvis or the Clash. Their opportunities to make any kind of an impression on television were so few and far between. They were always interviewed by a guy who was fifty years old, who had never heard of them. You'd rip your hair out watching it because everybody was just so clueless.

DAVE SIRULNICK Music videos you'd see on *The Midnight Special*, and *Don Kirshner's Rock Concert*, and *Video Jukebox*. HBO played videos between movies. The Beatles had done these things back in the '60s, when they didn't want to go on tour but they wanted to get some sort of promotional thing out there. There were a few of them for *American Bandstand*, who'd occasionally air something like this. They were these cool, three to four minutes, just totally off the wall, wild pieces.

JOHN SYKES The two most important forces in our lives were rock 'n' roll and television and that's why we wanted to start a music channel. Our parents couldn't understand it because they were thrilled just having three networks, and they had no connection with rock 'n' roll. For us, raised on three networks, we wanted more.

Origin

CHUCK D I saw a lot of Soft Cell, Thompson Twins, that type of stuff. Devo. A lot of Post-Brit-Punk English music—pop music at the time. I think it was the worst period of music ever. Between '79 and 1985, with the exception of Michael Jackson, Prince, and rap artists. Coincidentally, it was the beginning of MTV, so I know you guys ain't had a lot to work with.

MARTHA QUINN The idea for MTV in the early days was really a rock 'n' roll station on television. Twenty-four-hour clock, the rock 'n' roll mentality with the visual medium. The rock 'n' roll generation and the television age are just about the same age so it made sense that the two of those would be married.

JOHN SYKES In late 1980 I met Bob Pittman, who had just left WNBC in New York for Warner Amex to begin developing a music service. There was no MTV at that time—it was just called Music Program Development.

BOB PITTMAN, co-founder The concept was, "Let's alter the form of television to make it work for music." Because music is really about mood, emotion, attitude. TV is about a narrative story. So we sort of destroyed the narrative-story aspect of TV and really made it all about attitude.

JOHN MELLENCAMP I remember the first time I went to MTV, quite unsure of what it was, and I was one of the first guys there and was sitting in the waiting room with Graham Parker, and I looked at him and he looked at me and I said, "You know what this is?" And he says, "Yeah, they're gonna show videos all the time." We both kind of laughed and said, "That'll never work, nobody wants to watch them." We knew what these videos looked like up till that point. They were really terrible, silly, cheesy little productions.

JAY DORFMAN, promo producer, 1981 The early founders and creative team went against traditional instinct. Instead of hiring key television people, they hired people from a lot of nontelevision disciplines. So you got someone from radio, a copywriter from a travel magazine, a couple of young people with absolutely no idea what they were doing there. One guy who came in was working for his father in the dry-cleaning business.

TOM FRESTON, chairman and CEO One of the prerequisites for MTV was that you didn't have any experience, so you didn't bring any bad network TV habits with you. We had no money. If you had to take a taxi instead of a subway, that was a big deal in those days.

FRED SEIBERT, former executive It wasn't even called MTV back then. Warner Amex was developing several channels to be complements to the Movie Channel: the Games Channel, the Shopping Channel, and the Music Channel. But nobody likes a generic name. We sat down and tried to come up with some other names. Imagine if you sat down with your friends to come up with a name for a twenty-four-hour music channel. There were dozens, I remember Rock Box and TV1.

TOM FRESTON People would say things like, "This doesn't roll off the tongue, MTV." You get used to any name after a while, but it wasn't a popular choice.

FRED SEIBERT I went to a buddy of mine, Frank Olinsky, who loved rock 'n' roll. As kids, he introduced me to everyone from the Monkees to Frank Zappa. When he set up a graphic design studio in town, I knew he would be the right guy to do a logo.

TOM FRESTON That little company worked in a garage, one of several groups. People were sending in logos with musical notes and musical scales and all kinds of cliche things.

FRED SEIBERT A buddy of ours had written an article, the five greatest logos of all time: the Cross, the Star of David, the swastika, Coca-Cola, and CBS. We decided we needed to beat those five. We needed a trademark that was going to stand out. We also needed a logo that would be memorable enough, that people would remember to write it down in their ratings diaries.

FRANK OLINSKY, former executive Everything seemed too normal-looking. I suggested that the logo needed to be less corporate somehow, defaced or graffitied.

PATTI ROGOFF, designer I was walking to work one morning. I passed a school and a big brick fence that the kids had done a mural on. Somehow I'm thinking rock 'n' roll, strong, heavy duty. Television, changing, moving. I started sketching and I wound up with a tissue paper sketch of the block M, and the TV at that time was airbrushed, like graffiti.

FRED SEIBERT We went through several hundred logos. Finally at the bottom of the pile, there was a scrunched-up piece of tracing paper. It was literally the last one in the pile. And it was the M that we now know with a sort of scratched-in TV. We immediately said "this one." The team went and started experimenting with different ways to make it come alive.

FRANK OLINSKY I took an enlarged copy of the fat "M" drawing and went into the narrow stairwell with a piece of acetate and a can of black spray paint, and sprayed the "TV" lettering on it. We played around with the scale and proportion and after some tweaking arrived at the logo pretty much the way it appears today.

PATTI ROGOFF Very early on the concept was to make it move and change. We wanted the block heavy M, but the skin would change.

TOM FRESTON Everyone was appalled. No one had seen anything like this—hard to believe now. Our ad agency said we were about to make the biggest mistake we would ever make. We looked like we were a cinder block company.

FRED SEIBERT I really admired the people at Ogilvy and Mather. I walked in, and very proudly showed them the thing, and their faces all became glum. The head account guy leaves the room, comes back three minutes later with a typed piece of paper: "Ogilvy and Mather's rules for a good logo." We looked through it and we started checking it off. We broke nine out of ten. The creative director went to the head of our company and said this will be an absolute disaster, it will ruin your company.

GWEN STEFANI I remember all the animated MTV segments, like the one that turned into a beard.

On Air

MARK GOODMAN I just heard about this Warner Amex, they're doing this twenty-four-hour-a-day music video channel. Bob Pittman was involved, an interesting guy in radio at that time, the twenty-four-year-old whiz.

JOE DAVOLA, producer There weren't a lot of people and we would work around the clock. I mean we would work literally at 6:00 in the morning before we went on air. No one knew anything, we were making up the rules as we went. We did whatever we wanted. That was sort of the free-for-all chaos part of MTV.

J. J. JACKSON I almost didn't take the gig. And I would have killed myself afterward. We didn't know what this thing MTV was.

MARTHA QUINN When I first got what it was, it was like "Right! Okay! Twenty-four hours, radio, but on television. God, that makes sense! Why didn't I think of that?"

MARK GOODMAN We kind of dribbled in. Nina was hired first. Then J. J., and then me. And there was also this girl named Meg Griffin who was working in radio in New York. She had gotten the job. I remember taking a cab ride home with her and she was saying,

"Mark, I'm not doing this. This is never gonna happen." I said, "Meg, this is the biggest mistake of your life. You will regret this forever." She quit. Martha should be happy she quit, because Meg was the Martha Quinn type.

ALAN HUNTER They called up and said, "You're hired." And I said, "Hired for what? What in the hell *is* this show? Twenty-four hours a day of video? What?" I got the gig. They paid me a miserable salary, which, of course, to me was huge. They gave me a stack of videos a mile long and books to bone up on Def Leppard.

20 Questions for 20 Years

BRITNEY SPEARS

What song best describes your current state of mind?	"Gonna Make Me Lose My Mind Up in Here!"
What is favorite video of all time?	"Vogue"; Chris Isaak's "Wicked Game"
What is your first memory of MTV?	Seeing Michael Jackson's "Thriller"
Where were you the first time you saw yourself on MTV and how did you react?	"Baby..." on *TRL*—freaked out and jumped on the bed.
Does the video enhance or hinder the song?	Enhance
What is the most memorable moment you've witnessed on MTV?	MJ's VMA performance
Whose video work do you most admire?	Madonna
What do you like most about MTV?	It keeps me up on *all* sorts of music trends
What do you like least about MTV?	I love everything about MTV!
What is your favorite guilty pleasure video?	"Material Girl"
What do you consider to be MTV's greatest achievement and/or greatest failure in its first 20 years?	Providing a network that brings all genres of music together.
What is the worst reaction you've received to one of your videos?	Just not making it to #1 ever!
Videos should...	Be played more often—Ha ha! I'm a big fan of MTV2.
The best band name is	Butthole Surfers
The greatest moment in Rock and Pop and Rap was...	Michael Jackson on MTV
My biggest influence is	Madonna
My favorite VMA performance	Madonna's "Vogue" VMA performance
If I were president of MTV I would...	Be a very busy girl!
What artist would you most like to work with and what would you like to do with them?	Duet with Michael Jackson
Did video kill the radio star?	Absolutely not

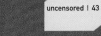

Launch

ANTHONY KIEDIS I remember going "Whoa! Music on TV. What's going on? Dude, check this out, look what they're doing here. What channel is this?"

ALAN HUNTER The first night that MTV went on the air, it was a total blast. We had taped a day or two ahead. We had been rehearsing for three weeks. So the night of the big launch, we were gonna have a big party out in Joisey.

MARK GOODMAN They loaded us on a bus to bring us to Fort Lee, New Jersey. There are people upstairs at this restaurant having dinner, they're like ninety years old. And we're downstairs in this basement. A million people and some cheesy hors d'oeuvres.

ALAN HUNTER They picked this dump of a place, like a bad Holiday Inn banquet room. They had a big TV and all of us herded in there. There were so many people involved in the beginning, about a hundred, who didn't even know each other. This was like the first coming together of the office workers and studio people. No one even knew who the VJs were. It was like, "What do you do for the company?" "I'm up there, on the screen." "Oh, hey, how you doing?"

MARK GOODMAN The five of us were just incredibly excited. Nervous. Nina was wearing something really sexy that night. I actually teared up when that rocket took off. We had been working so hard on this for like four weeks before we actually went on the air. And it never felt like it was gonna happen.

ALAN HUNTER It was July 31. 11:59. It's coming up on midnight. And we had heard the opening piece, the rocket segment, but it had never been seen, out there in "the world." At twelve o'clock—*boom!*—the rocket blasts off. Buggles come on. "Video Killed the Radio Star." The first part of the Buggles song still gives me tingles. When that was over, I thought, "And now we're gonna be on." All five of us were out of our brains.

PAT BENATAR There were like five videos and that's all there were. And they played them twenty-four hours a day—it was nuts. MTV changed everything as we knew it.

MARK GOODMAN It was incredibly moving.

BOB PITTMAN As soon as we launched, everything went wrong. So I immediately went to the telephone. I was on the phone to the network operations center. And we were talking through almost every piece of the service through the rest of the night.

ALAN HUNTER Each of us did a piece of script, when we shot. "Welcome to MTV, blah blah." First Mark, then Nina, Martha, J. J., and me at the end. They had put the segment in the wrong order and I got put in first by mistake. So as a matter of trivia, I was the first VJ to show up on MTV—by accident.

BOB PITTMAN The videos all got out of sequence so the VJ segment was saying, "And that was," and that wasn't what was played before. And "This is . . ." and that's not what this is. Audio wasn't going through. Pictures weren't coming through.

ALAN HUNTER Oh my God. This is getting off to an auspicious start.

TOM PETTY When I first saw it, I didn't know how long it was going to be on that day so I must have sat there six hours waiting for that show to end and it just kept going, over and over. And I liked it. I thought, this is going to be interesting.

First Videos

Buggles	"Video Killed the Radio Star"	Robert Palmer	"Looking for Clues"
Pat Benatar	"You Better Run"	Shoes	"Too Late"
Rod Stewart	"She Won't Dance with Me"	Stevie Nicks with Tom Petty and the Heartbreakers	"Stop Draggin' My Heart Around"
The Who	"You Better You Bet"		
PH.D.	"Little Susie's on the Up"	Rupert Hine	"Surface Tension"
Cliff Richard	"We Don't Talk Anymore"	Split Enz	"One Step Ahead"
Pretenders	"Brass in Pocket"	Gerry Rafferty	"Baker Street"
Todd Rundgren	"Time Heals"	Pat Benatar	"Turn It On Like I Do"
REO Speedwagon	"Take It on the Run"	Tom Johnston	"Savannah Nights"
Styx	"Rockin' the Paradise"	Rockestra	"Lucille"
Robin Lane and the Chartbusters	"When Things Go Wrong"	Styx	"The Best of Times"
		Carly Simon	"Vengeance"
Split Enz	"History Never Repeats"	Iron Maiden	"Wrathchild"
.38 Special	"Hold on Loosely"	Blotto	"I Wanna Be a Lifeguard"
April Wine	"Just Between You and Me"	Rod Stewart	"Passion"
Rod Stewart	"Sailing"	Elvis Costello	"Oliver's Army"
Iron Maiden	"Iron Maiden"	REO Speedwagon	"Don't Let Him Go"
REO Speedwagon	"Keep on Loving You"	The Silencers	"Remote Control"/ "I'm Too Illegal"
Pretenders	"Message of Love"		
Lee Ritenour	"Mr. Briefcase"	Juice Newton	"Angel of the Morning"
The Cars	"Double Life"	Rockpile	"Little Sister"
Phil Collins	"In the Air Tonight"	Bootcamp	"Hold on to the Night"

Cliff Richard	"Dreaming"
Lee Ritenour	"Is It You"
Fleetwood Mac	"Tusk"
Michael Stanley	"He Can't Love You"
REO Speedwagon	"Tough Guys"
Blondie	"Rapture"
The Who	"Don't Let Go the Coat"
Rod Stewart	"Ain't Love a Bitch"
Pretenders	"Talk of the Town"
Rainbow	"Can't Happen Here"
Andrew Gold	"Thank You for Being a Friend"
Gerry Rafferty	"Bring It All Home"
April Wine	"Sign of the Gypsy"
Kate Bush	"The Man with the Child in His Eyes"
David Bowie	"Ashes to Ashes"
April Wine	"Just Between You and Me"
The Specials	"Rat Race"
Talking Heads	"Once in a Lifetime"
Bootcamp	"Victim"
Rod Stewart	"Tonight's the Night"
Nick Lowe	"Cruel to Be Kind"

Buggles
"Video Killed The Radio Star"
The Age Of Plastic
ISLAND RECORDS

L.L. Cool J Unplugged

BUSTA RHYMES That was my first time seeing a live band with a rapper and it was incredible. It was so hot how he controlled the band and they doped it up and he sped up with it, that was really really hot.

ALEX COLETTI, executive producer L.L. shows up, gets onstage, and you thought the guy has led a band his entire life. He just jumped in, started calling out changes and it just clicked. He wouldn't even stop between songs. Boom, boom, boom, and you just felt it. The only part where L.L. slipped up and had to stop and retake it, he said, "Rewind that. Oh, I mean, play that over."

B REAL It was the first time that any established rapper or hard-core rapper, which, at the time he was still considered, came out with a live band and rocked it and did it well. Another thing that stood out was when he put his arms up and his deodorant was just all over the place. Maybe that one we shouldn't want to remember.

ALEX COLETTI L.L. was a little sweaty. He needed some deodorant. So I sent somebody. He basically snapped a stick of Right Guard in half and slapped it under each arm and that was fine until he took his shirt off. But it was the most fierce performance. People were standing and dancing in the aisles. L.L. ripped his shirt off and Pop ripped his shirt off and someone in the audience ripped their shirt off and this was just a throwdown.

TED DEMME, producer *Yo! MTV Raps* When L.L. did "Mama Said Knock You Out," I don't think I ever bopped so hard to anything in my life. It was the most energetic live performance I'd seen. He just exploded. L.L. just hit another level after that. For L.L. to come out and do that song with a band, it was arguably one of the first kind of live hip-hop shows broadcast. It probably influenced a lot of musicians to start playing with live bands after that.

EVE We are artists too, we are entertainers too, and we should be able to show that side. Rap artists can share the same stage with a rock band. Why not?

ROBERT SMALL, co-creator/executive producer of *Unplugged* When you saw L.L. doing his thing, it was really unplugged. It showed the fact that his music had something going for it that people didn't previously give it credit for.

OPPOSITE
Plugged in at
the Video Music
Awards 1996

Early Days

MARILYN MANSON I was completely obsessed with it. I watched it every day. There were probably only five videos that they played. I remember just being so excited by the idea.

MARK GOODMAN After day one, it was just like: Feed the beast. MTV consumed everything that you did. Every interview, every day on the air was this huge behemoth to try to keep running.

TOM MORELLO My earliest memory of MTV is not having it. My family was about the last to have cable on the block so I'd have to stop by friends' houses after school. We'd have little cable-watching parties. It was always very tragic because I was interested in the new rocking April Wine video when they were more psyched to see Talk Talk or Haircut 100. So they'd always lobby to change the channel when Def Leppard's "Photograph" came on and I was riveted to try to see how he was fretting the notes.

JOHN SYKES, former executive I remember driving around with Tom Freston in Tulsa, Oklahoma, looking for a story on MTV that we could use in the trades, and we finally found this store that sold a box of Buggles albums. Within three weeks we had

full-page ads in every music sheet in America saying MTV sells records. That was the first success story we had. We went back to the record companies and said, "Make more videos, we help you."

BILLY CORGAN If you came home from school or in the middle of the night you could watch it. As a kid, it made music seem more glamorous.

TOM FRESTON, chairman and CEO You would see the impact MTV had had really quite clearly. We tried to document that. There was major awareness right away, selling a lot of records by groups like Squeeze or English Beat or the Buggles. People were getting Rod Stewart haircuts. There was a frenzy. Radio stations were getting requests for songs no one had ever heard of.

LARS ULRICH My earliest memory of MTV is sittin' around Dave Mustaine's apartment in Huntington Beach. There wasn't a lot of stuff on other than music videos at the time. I don't know if anybody out there who watches MTV today can relate to that.

JOHN SYKES At that time, the record companies had no interest in spending the money on promoting the bands in another arena. They thought radio was just fine.

PINK *Remote Control* was my earliest memory of MTV. I used to love *Remote Control*. I got grounded for watching MTV. I don't think I was allowed to watch it 'til I was like thirteen or fourteen. My mom said it was nasty, and now I'm on it.

ROB THOMAS We couldn't afford MTV. We didn't have cable but my mom's boyfriend did. I would sneak over there, hang out, sit in there mesmerized by MTV.

LENNY KRAVITZ I remember watching Prince. "Wow, there he is." I can see him. I remember when Michael Jackson first came on. "Billie Jean." I don't know if that was the first black video but I remember before that there weren't any black videos on.

SLASH I'd sit there after getting back from rehearsal, watching MTV till I fell asleep.

TOM FRESTON We were always fighting for our space. We were always trying to get respect for MTV because the big network guys were out there getting first dibs because they had all the money. We were out there trying to convince everybody that we were more powerful because we could expose the music. Once we started to break bands like the Police, Duran Duran, and Billy Idol, and Madonna, people started to see the cause and effect of playing their videos on the channel.

SIMON LeBON Well, I don't remember first seeing MTV. I think we were on it before we saw it. I remember I was at home in the U.K. and there was a news story on Radio 1 about this new music channel, twenty-four hours of music videos, in the States. I thought, *Wow this is great.* The next minute the phone rings, I pick it up, and it's the damn DJ from the radio station. He says, "Simon, from Duran Duran, I've got you on the air. What do you think about this MTV thing?" I said, "Well, isn't it just great. You can just use it like the old radio. Just turn it on when you want to." And now you can't live without it.

ALAN HUNTER What made us all bond was our damn dressing room. In the early days of MTV, we were lean and mean. We had one little room. They herded us in there and said, "This is where it is." We had five little racks in one little corner and we were all supposed to do our thing in there. We got really close. There was a little alcove where the mirror was. Right around the alcove was the dressing area. When we had a little crossover, I'm putting my makeup on, Nina's right over there putting her clothes on. It was ridiculous. But we very quickly became brothers and sisters.

MARK GOODMAN We absolutely felt we were in the trenches together. None of us had really had a ton of experience with television. We felt like we had this dramatic camaraderie. We were putting on a show. We got to be there for twelve and thirteen and fourteen hours a day.

MARTHA QUINN We pretty much made it a point to see the videos. Sometimes you would get caught and there would be a world premiere video that would be edited literally at the last minute and would go out to the satellite uplink center, so nobody would have seen it. You would just have to go, "Wow, all right, the Rolling Stones," and for all you knew, the last shot was all of them decapitated and in flames and babies dying.

J. J. JACKSON MTV wisely sat us down and told us that life was going to change for us drastically when MTV went on in Manhattan. They were absolutely right. Within a month of going on the air in Manhattan, I had to move.

STEVE LEEDS, talent executive Julie Brown and Adam Curry were the two biggest stars on the channel, in the late '80s. They were both very highly paid. They were both very well taken care of by the channel. But they both believed their own personas

were real. Julie had people kowtowing to her from a fashion point of view. And Adam was just a celebrity who everybody wanted to meet. So, while they had some commonality, in that they both had this celebrity star status, being VJs, they did not necessarily get along the best behind the scenes.

I don't think anybody ever knew that, but I knew well enough not to leave them in closed quarters together because inevitably they'd get into a spat, of something of the most ridiculous nature. We pumped these people up here at the channel and made them believe they were special and uniquely talented. And so it was inevitable that those kinds of attitudes would come out.

ADAM CURRY I have a theory about MTV. They never wanted the VJs to be stars—ever. But at the same time they wanted everybody to be irreverent and recognizable and noticeable enough.

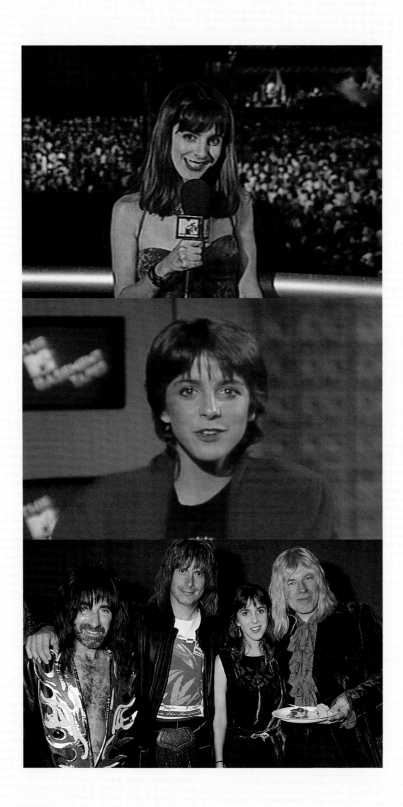

Martha Quinn

1981–86

JON STEWART Martha Quinn, let's face facts, was America's sweetheart. We all had a little crush on her. I don't know if it was the dope, or how late it was, but she was a very adorable, pixieish young lady. And could introduce a video like nobody's business. And who else were you going to have a crush on at the time? J. J. Jackson?

JOHN NORRIS A lot of us hadn't really seen MTV yet, but the big story at my dorm was the fact that one of the alumni from the NYU dorm had become one of the original VJs at MTV. She used to hand out light-bulbs and toilet paper at the front desk. And two months later she was a star on cable.

MARTHA QUINN I was an intern at WNBC [radio in NYC] with "Pig Vomit" [the general manager of Howard Stern fame] right before Howard was there. Bob Pittman used to be the program director before he left to go start this weird cable channel. Somebody calls Bob Pittman, it's 5:30 in the afternoon. They say there's this girl here who used to be our intern. She should be a VJ. Next thing I know, I was in a cab going to MTV studios. I had no makeup on. I had a T-shirt that my college roommate had given me. I auditioned. Two days later I got the job. I had to quit my job at the dormitory.

MARK GOODMAN I had the hots for Martha for a while.

MARTHA QUINN We hit the ground running. It was, "Hey kids, let's put on a show." People would stop me and say, "What're you doing?" I would just have to go, "Well, uh, I'm working on this cable station. It's videos. It's twenty-four hours. I'm a VJ—it's like being a DJ, but it's on television."

JON STEWART She was the girl. Nina Blackwood seemed unattainable. Mythological if you will. Martha Quinn seemed like the girl that would turn you down at your own college.

MARTHA QUINN My first interview ever—ever— was Simon and Garfunkel. Hello, could you give me someone smaller? Could you give me an intro artist?

J. J. JACKSON Martha became my baby sister. I always looked out for her.

MARTHA QUINN I really considered MTV my job. I took it really seriously. I didn't go out partying. I didn't jet around with rock stars. I was too busy studying. I would read rock encyclopedias from cover to cover. I wish I had gone back and gone out and gone to clubs.

Working—The '80s

DOUG HERZOG, former executive It was the most fun you could have at work with your clothes on. All these great people, working real hard, coming up with crazy ideas on a Monday, and putting it on the air on Wednesday, working our asses off, just having a ball, really.

JANEANE GAROFALO Now MTV is absolutely dominating the world. But before they would pull a lot of creative types from like Emerson College, pay them five dollars a week and just get all of their creativity and ideas and then these kids would leave. Because they'd be like, "I can't live on five dollars a week."

ALISON STEWART My job was the care and feeding of Downtown Julie Brown, Adam Curry, and Kevin Seal. I had just graduated from Brown University with my fancy seventy-five-thousand-dollar degree. I was calling commuter cars and putting water on the set. It was my first job. When I interviewed for the job, Kevin Seal walked in in his underpants. Kevin's a little furry and he just sort of said, "Oh, hi, how you doing, it's nice to meet you." I didn't really flinch and the gentleman I was interviewing with said, "Okay, you can have the job."

TED DEMME When I started at MTV, around '85, our bosses were in their twenties. I was a production assistant in the promo department. It was really my film school. I learned every facet of production. You'd go and get lunch, you'd answer the phones, you'd learn how to get on the computer, you'd learn how to talk politely on the phone, you'd meet talent. You just did everything.

Eventually, someone would get sick, and there would be an editing session happening. They'd go, "All right Ted, here you go. Run to the editing session." And the next thing you knew you were in an online session. Next thing you knew you were on a shoot interviewing a rock star, cutting an ID, cutting a promo. It was amazing, the opportunities.

DEBBIE LIEBLING, former production executive I remember joking right before I took the job, "Oh before you know it, I'll be best friends with Dee Snider," who was on the charts at the time. And wouldn't you know it, my first week, there I get booked on the shoot with Twisted Sister, and I'm sitting there with Dee Snider.

LAUREN LAZIN, executive producer On my first day, I remember being concerned about what I should wear. It was the '80s, so I was really into miniskirts and go-go boots. I really wanted to work in television but I didn't want to work anyplace that was gonna be too corporate. At the same time, I didn't want to come in too trendy. So I just came to work in what I thought was a really cute outfit. And I remember walking in and feeling totally, completely comfortable. Everyone felt like someone I could've hung out with in college.

COLIN QUINN Nobody had an idea of what was going to go on. Everybody would be looking at each other, hoping somebody would say something funny, fast. It was more the vibe of the time. Just going on trips together, you couldn't help but get really close to people because you were always out, always together.

DAVID FELTON, writer The best thing was that you could just go up to the boss and say, "How's this?" and she'd say, "Great, go do it." The creative process was very direct and hands-on. There were all these creative people working together.

JOE DAVOLA Everybody worked really hard, but everybody partied really hard. It was really a family. We all moved in packs.

1775 broadway
mtv headquarters
10-13-88

J. J. JACKSON The wonderful thing about MTV was the opportunity—which still exists there—is that you could see kids who aren't on camera, really grow. I saw a lot of people who are now heavy hitters grow, who started out as gofers.

TED DEMME MTV is the only place you could think of an idea on Monday, you could get it approved Tuesday, you would write it on Wednesday, you'd shoot it Thursday, you'd cut it Friday and it would air Saturday. And it might suck and it might be great, I had no idea, and if it sucked, who cares? So what? It was on for an hour, you would never see it again.

ALEX COLLETTI In 1987, MTV was really simple. There were three associate producers and we did all the VJ segments. At that point everything was VJ segments. Twenty-four hours a day, seven days a week, no shows except VJ segments. No *Real World*, game shows, *Remote Control* was just in its infancy. We did music videos 24/7. You were in the studio every other day with all the VJs that were on the air, in that order. Adam would come in the morning and then Julie and Carolyn. You'd work with five or six of

them in the course of a day. The next day at the office you get the music, prep some stuff. The next day back in the studio.

KEN OBER It was such an amazing place to work. Especially if you're a freeloader like myself. I mean, the free stuff at MTV...I don't think I paid for a shirt, pair of sneakers, concert ticket, a drink, or dinner for seven years. You would hear about a concert, Eric Clapton or Van Halen or whatever. Bing, one phone call, boom, you're at the show.

DEBBIE LIEBLING I did a number of things with Frank Zappa. I was at his house in L.A. shooting. I started to feel like, "Hey Frank, I'm here. I know where the ketchup is." You really got to know the people over time.

ED LOVER It was real, everybody was more open. It's a little more corporate now for me.

DR. DRE We took a lot of chances back then.

ALLIE EBERHARDT, producer When Bono or Van Halen or Axel Rose would come up to the offices you saw them. Because they had to walk through the halls.

KEN OBER I was an old rock 'n' roll guy when I got the job and MTV really did expose me to new music. A couple of people in the talent department would always make me these tapes. It would help my music education. It got me away from the Who and the Stones a little.

J. J. JACKSON We were all close. Plus we were at Thirty-third Street and Tenth, which is kind of a sleazy section. A lot of hookers. There was a little diner there and that was it. We were either at the studio or at that diner, because if you ventured beyond that, you were in a really bad section.

TOM FRESTON It was a heady time and there were a lot of people who got kind of full of themselves thinking they were geniuses. There were a lot of people who sort of burnt out along the trail, just working too hard, or the classic kind of drugs and booze and just erratic, obsessive behavior, some of which just seemed kind of funny at the time. We took some casualties.

VMA 1991

DATE September 5
LOCATION Universal Amphitheatre, Los Angeles
HOST Arsenio Hall

PERFORMERS

Guns N' Roses	"Live and Let Die"
Don Henley	"Heart of the Matter"
L.L. Cool J	"Mama Said Knock You Out"
Metallica	"Enter Sandman"
Prince and the New Power Generation	"Gett Off"
Van Halen	"Poundcake"
C+C Music Factory	"Things That Make You Go Hmmm"/"Here We Go"/ "Gonna Make You Sweat (Everybody Dance Now)" (medley)
Mariah Carey	"Emotions"
Paula Abdul	"Vibeology"
EMF	"Unbelievable"
Poison	"Unskinny Bop"
Queensrÿche	"Silent Lucidity"

WINNERS

Best Video	R.E.M., "Losing My Religion"
Best Male Video	Chris Isaak, "Wicked Game"
Best Female Video	Janet Jackson, "Love Will Never Do Without You"
Best Group Video	R.E.M., "Losing My Religion"
Best Rap Video	L.L. Cool J, "Mamma Said Knock You Out"
Best Dance Video	C+C Music Factory, "Gonna Make You Sweat (Everybody Dance Now)"
Best Metal/Hard Rock Video	Aerosmith, "The Other Side"
Best Alternative Music Video	Jane's Addiction, "Been Caught Stealing"
Best New Artist	Jesus Jones, "Right Here, Right Now"
Breakthrough Video	R.E.M., "Losing My Religion"
Michael Jackson's Video Vanguard	Bon Jovi and Wayne Isham
Viewer's Choice	Queensrÿche, "Silent Lucidity"

Heard Any Good Jokes Lately?

JOEL GALLEN, producer The 1991 VMAs will always be remembered for Pee Wee Herman. Earlier in the year he was caught doing whatever he was doing in a movie theater. It was a big controversy on the front page of all the papers. Just a great opportunity for MTV to seize the moment.

CHRIS KRESKI, writer Right after that happened we said, "We should bring him to the Video Music Awards." Judy McGrath said it would be nice to give him some sort of high-profile "welcome back where he would be among friends. He's a creative genius, after all."

JOEL GALLEN We track down his lawyer and talk to his publicist. At first they said there's no possible way. But we were relentless.

CHRIS KRESKI The day before the show, Pee Wee agreed to do it. He was gonna roll up in a limousine, get out, get onstage, say his one line and get out.

JOEL GALLEN I talked to him on the phone before the show and the first thing he said to me was, "You know what I'm thinking? I think I'm just going to walk out there and say, "Hey, have you heard any good jokes lately?'" At the time, you couldn't go anywhere without someone telling a Pee Wee joke.

I immediately said, "That's exactly what you should say." And he said, "Well, why don't you get your writers to write up a bunch of other ideas?" So we did and we wrote up like fifty other ideas. He said he had a few other thoughts and that he was going to decide right before he walked out onstage!

JUDY MCGRATH, president, MTV group and chairman interactive music I remember saying a quick hello to Pee Wee then going back out to the last couple of rows to watch it happen. Herzog had been dealing with all this drama from Van Halen, who wanted to go first and open the show cold. But the night belonged to Pee Wee. He got a very emotional response. Instant standing and building ovation. Some people were saying, "Is that really him? A lookalike? Could it be...?" Everyone just cheered and cheered. He was gone in a flash.

JOEL GALLEN Prince had this idea where it was almost like staging an orgy. They cast like fifty to sixty people from the L.A. area and they rehearsed it and built this enormous set, kind of like a harem with fire and people performing simulated sex acts. A lot of times the artist or his record company would help pay the cost of production, because MTV had a budget and Prince was one of those guys who wanted to be so good they will go into their own pockets.

That is how much of a commitment he was making to try and make an impact with his performance. He also didn't tell us what he was going to wear. So he's out there playing his electric yellow guitar and all of a sudden he turns around and his butt cheeks are showing.

CHRIS KRESKI We knew it was going to be something like that. We didn't know the pants had no back in that part. That was the surprise nobody knew. There were a million dancers and they didn't have much on in rehearsal either.

Mark Goodman

1981–87

MARK GOODMAN In the beginning, we weren't on in New York City. People would ask me what I was doing. I'd say, "I swear to God, I'm working. I swear, I'm famous in Cheyenne, Wyoming." All of us would go to a concert in New Jersey and we'd be like the Beatles. We'd come back to Manhattan, trying to get into a club, and they'd be looking behind us to see who else should be getting in.

First time we went to Cheyenne, we got the full-on limo from the airport to take us to the hotel. Palatial room. Everybody just making sure that "Mr. Goodman" was really comfortable. We got into the limo to go to our appearance at the record store. I thought somebody else was appearing there because so many people were there. I'm like, "Who's here?" It was me!

At first we never got to see the videos. We would tape in advance in the studio. I started to fight to be able to see the reels of music videos that were being shown. We'd be saying, "Wow! Here's a new Pat Benatar song." But we never heard it. We never saw it. I don't know nothing about it, but wasn't that great? So I fought to get the tape sent down so we would be able to watch them.

When Van Halen fired David Lee Roth, David and I wound up having this weird conversation in the men's room of a hotel. We were in there for an hour and a half, just sitting on the sink. We both sort of acknowledged the fact that we were both Jewish . . . He kind of just dropped the whole David Lee Roth thing and became Dave. He's such a smart guy, genuinely fun. Really funny.

My time at MTV was the center of the universe. I'm amazed at the places people spring up to tell me what a big part of their childhood or college life I was. In retrospect, I have come to respect what we did. It was a lot harder than I imagined. I feel good that I was a part of the culture.

New Year's Eve

FIRST NEW YEAR'S EVE ROCK 'N' ROLL BALL

PERFORMANCES Karla DeVito, Bow Wow Wow, and David Johansen

VINNIE LONGOBARDO, executive producer We did the first New Year's Eve show basically just a few months after we went on the air. They invited more people than they should have. I guess they were afraid that not enough people would show up because people didn't know what MTV was. So we wound up having a very overpacked auditorium, and it was a lot of fun. David Johansen played and he was great.

In the early days we did all the New Year's Eve shows live. We started the show at around eleven, eleven-thirty, and went until four o'clock in the morning. And that makes for a nice, long, wild party, and the longer it went on the wilder it got, because people would just keep drinking and drinking and drinking.

JUDY MCGRATH It was pouring outside. People were lined up for blocks, getting soaked, trying to get into this MTV party at this crazy old hotel, Diplomat. I think they tore the place down a few months later. I remember seeing John Belushi in a stairwell, and Keith Haring, who had designed the graphics for the show, dancing wildly, all the early 1980s art and music and comedy people coming together. It was a heady mix. I thought, *Wow, I guess this thing is going to work.*

Shake and Squirt

DAVID BERRENT, producer I remember in 1987, the Beastie Boys were performing and I didn't know who the Beastie Boys were. It was another crowded, crazy show. I was jammed up at the front of the stage, holding cue cards for whoever introduced them. I guess back in those days MTV couldn't afford a TelePrompTer. So they intro'd the Beastie Boys and out they came, shaking up their beer, squirting beer on people. People started stage-diving and moshing. Someone stole one of the Beasties' microphones and then fistfights started breaking out and somehow I got in the middle of this brawl. One of the big security guards put me in a head lock and started pummeling me. I hold up my badge, let him know I'm like, "I'm on your side."

Looking back on it, I guess it was pretty funny. But at the time, I didn't want to be there getting smashed around.

VINNIE LONGOBARDO The Beastie Boys were the bad boys of MTV at the time. Anything you weren't supposed to do on TV, they did.

Target Practice

VINNIE LONGOBARDO I think they wanted some kind of big visual moment to show that it was New Year's

Eve, and, you know, dropping balloons was pretty clichéd. Unfortunately, no one ever thought about the idea that once you drop Ping-Pong balls, they're available for everyone to pick up and start throwing.

RENE GARCIA, producer Starship played that year. They were kind of our headliners. And after all those Ping-Pong balls fell from the ceiling, someone announced the band. And nothing happened.

Somebody told me that Starship was doing a chant backstage, sort of, "Ohhhmmm, we're all together, we're getting ready to go on! Ohhhmmm!" And their chanting had sort of taken too long or something, and they missed their cue. So when they came out, the audience expressed their displeasure at being made to wait.

Now, you gotta realize, this audience was pretty rowdy. Guys in suits were bombed out of their minds and throwing Ping-Pong balls at the band. And they didn't appreciate this. They were like ready to walk off, but they were troupers. They stuck it out. And they were getting beaned with Ping-Pong balls for pretty much the whole set.

VINNIE LONGOBARDO I know Mickey Thomas and Grace Slick were pretty pissed off. So, it was a fiasco for the producers who had to deal with a very irate band when they got off the stage.

CARSON DALY Billie Joe [Green Day] was just good and liquored up. I remember my dressing room here, which is really like a broom closet, was where all of the bands were coming to smoke and drink. It was like this little Studio 54 VIP room, with the most random people. I remember coming in at one moment that night to sit down for a second and catch my breath, and there was Billie Joe waxed out, some Playmate, my buddy from L.A., and someone else's mom. It was like the weirdest little group in there. And they're all eating carrots. It was just so random. The shit that you saw that night was crazy.

But I know he was good and liquored up and he was trying to sing "Time of Your Life" and I was onstage, now that I think about it, and he was just inebriated. He couldn't sing and he could barely play the chords. And the next thing I know he's outside in Times Square climbing scaffolding.

TOMMY CODY, writer Marilyn Manson was soundchecking the night before MTV's New Year's Eve 2001 show, and after they went through a couple songs, Marilyn asked Twiggy Ramirez what he thought would happen if he [Marilyn] slammed into the window of the Times Square studios. I saw Twiggy make a hand gesture like, "You'd go straight through, straight *down*, and crash onto the sidewalk." Marilyn nodded his head. He agreed.

At the next night's performance, during the guitar solo of the first song, Marilyn took about a ten-foot running start, and smashed himself right into the glass. It didn't break, he obviously didn't go through, and there was no harm done—but all I could think about was how he'd already figured that he'd go through. He was either really into "the moment," or he has absolutely no regard for his own safety.

It was their first song of the night.

While Marilyn Manson was playing a cover version of Cheap Trick's "Surrender" on the New Year's Eve 2001 show, I was sitting in the control room next to [executive producer] Dave Sirulnick. Marilyn was getting a bit out of control onstage, especially with his handling of the mic stand. Dave got on the headset to the floor manager and told him to get the security guys ready. "If Manson picks that thing up like a baseball bat, I want security to tackle him if he gets even an *inch* closer to the audience." After a second, Dave added, "I don't care if he starts swinging at the other guys in the band, though."

Alan Hunter

1981–87

ALAN HUNTER When I got out of college, I said to hell with psychology. I decided to just go to New York and pursue my acting dream.

Nine months later, I had just gotten through doing the new wave punk rock version of *A Midsummer Night's Dream*, off-off-off-off-Broadway, down in an East Fourth Street theater. I was wearing tights and no shirt, prancing around as an asexual spirit of the forest. I was in *Annie*, the movie. I was in a David Bowie music video, "Fashion."

I met Bob Pittman at a social function, went and auditioned about a month and a half before it went on the air, in June 1981. I did the world's worst audition. I just didn't know how to talk extemporaneously. I was surprised that, two weeks later, they called me and said, "We'd like you back again." I said, "To hell with you. More punishment?"

They had the black guy, they had the Jew, they had the dumb blonde gal, they had the cutesy little Martha. They needed the airhead blond Midwestern guy.

The first six months were hell for me. I couldn't quite get into the swing of being myself on camera. I was still trying to be an actor. I could see them every day just going, "Oh, God, we made a mistake. We've hired the wrong guy."

The first month I was on the air, I continued to bartend. We weren't on in Manhattan. The second week, I was making a daiquiri for this guy from Jersey. He's sitting there, looking at me, going, "I know this guy." That was the first time I went, "I don't know him, why would he know me?" Three or four months later, Nina and I are waiting for a taxi and this guy drives up. "Oh my God! You're Nina Blackwood." I think it started with her. And the guy looked at me and said, "And you're Mark Hunter!" Mark Hunter? I decked him.

J. J. Jackson

1981–86

J. J. JACKSON I was living in L.A. After the audition they came up and said, "We can't guarantee anything, but you are a front-runner." I was happy about it. Then they said, "You'll move to New York." I literally slid down the wall. They said, "What's wrong?" I showed them the mountains and the sky. This doesn't exist in Manhattan.

I was a little intimidated by Manhattan. I'm just by myself. But everyone took me under their wing, even the receptionist.

Early on, Muddy Waters died. MTV was doing meager coverage of that event and was doing a big buildup of Spandau Ballet. I thought MTV didn't have a lot of credibility that first week. I said to myself, "God damn it—I sold out."

I didn't even know little Martha, and if you can imagine, she's on a college campus, and I'm a grown man. She actually called up to my hotel room and asked if she could come see me. I don't know her from nothing. She comes up and says, "Look, if you don't mind me saying this: I think you may just be a little homesick and a little intimidated by this city. And you're right in what you had to say today. And maybe they should have given it more coverage. But I think that you're blowing it a bit out of proportion." She says, "I may be out of line saying this to you, but I think if you walk away and leave this, you're gonna be awfully sorry."

I said, "Okay, kid. Let's go have some dinner." We went to dinner and she became my little sister after that.

"Pot party in my room," said Krist Novoselic, with a beery chortle. Looking back now, I realize I should have just walked away.

It was December 1993, and Nirvana bassist Novoselic and his bandmates were passing through St. Paul, Minnesota, on tour. Soldiering along as opening acts were two of Nirvana's favorite groups: the Breeders, led by ex-Pixie Kim Deal, and the wonderful all-girl Japanese punk band Shonen Knife.

At MTV News around that time, we were always up for covering Nirvana, a truly great rock band. This time, though, there was a problem: the group had already done a bunch of press for this tour, and didn't want to do any more. But since MTV producer Michael Alex and I were also fans of Shonen Knife, we tried to sell our bosses on the idea of taking advantage of this rare Stateside visit to interview the lovable trio before they (as we dementedly thought) blew up huge and conquered the world. (Or at least that part of it composed of import-record collectors and international whimsy aficionados.)

Unfortunately, it was the end of the year, and we were told there was no money left in the News budget to finance a road trip just to cover a Japanese cult band. So we tried an end run, and put our case directly to Nirvana: If we could somehow arrange to come out on the road, ostensibly to do a report on Shonen Knife, might Nirvana agree to make itself available for an interview too? The bosses would buy that.

Nirvana, affable as always, said sure. Frontman Kurt Cobain was a huge fan of Shonen Knife's sweet, Ramones-like songs about ice cream, jelly beans, and butterfly boys, and he adored having them along on his tour. ("I cried every night," he told us later.)

So off we flew to Minneapolis. We interviewed Shonen Knife (they were so cute: they'd just discovered the joys of Black Sabbath) and then, true to their word, Nirvana turned up. The boys put away a considerable amount of beer before the interview ended, and after Cobain decided to retire to his room for the night, I found myself in Novoselic's digs, helping him and auxiliary guitarist Pat Smear deplete the room-service red-wine supply. Things started going seriously downhill when the two of them began rolling around on the floor doing their faux gay-boys-in-heat act. ("I don't go all the way!" Pat yelped at one point, sucking his tongue back out of Novoselic's mouth.) Then Krist got up and lifted a sizable mirror off a wall hook and hurled it across the room. It hit the opposite wall with a crash, and we watched in sudden, stunned silence as its glittering shards tinkled onto the carpet. Soon the air was filled with flying tables and chairs (and loud, maniacal laughter), and the floor was littered with wreckage. I did my best imitation of a neutral, disinterested observer.

It was about four in the morning when the phone rang: hotel security was on the way up. I took this opportunity to slip out of the wrecked room and make my way down the hall to an elevator—where I was startled to be joined almost immediately by Smear and Novoselic, the two of them cackling like loons. It seemed we were now all on our way to . . . my room.

There, things got considerably uglier, with much breakage ensuing. (Since I had no desire to play the cop at this destructathon, my objections, I have to admit, were of only the mildest variety.) At one point, Novoselic lifted up a heavy wooden coat stand and, gripping the thing like a medieval jousting lance, attempted to ram it through the screen of the room's TV set—which turned out to be much more difficult to do than you might imagine. Then, suddenly, both he and Smear were gone, and standing in their place was a deeply unamused hotel security bruiser, staring around at the ruin of my room (at the light fixtures dangling pathetically from the ceiling, among many other things), with a look of withering disgust on his face.

The next few hours were utilized by Nirvana's equally unamused Scottish road manager to berate his errant charges in the angriest possible way. What were they doing, he hissed furiously, running around acting like . . . *like fookin' Guns N' Roses or something?* (In other words, like exactly the sort of ostentatiously decadent rock stars for whom they had always professed such contempt.)

Checkout, a few hours later, was a mopey process, complicated by industrial-strength hangovers. The damages assessed by the hotel amounted to some $18,000, if I remember right, and Nirvana got the bill. (Note to aspiring room-wreckers: the afflicted hotel will charge you not only for the actual damage you've done, but for whatever it estimates to be the amount of rental revenue it stands to lose while repairs are under way in the rooms you trashed.)

I'm not an endorser of mindless destruction, but the unrehearsed spontaneity of this particular incident was oddly refreshing, given what I'd come to learn was the generally overcontrolled context of the average TV assignment.

—KURT LODER

VMA 1985

DATE September 13
LOCATION Radio City Music Hall, New York
HOST Eddie Murphy

HIGHLIGHTS
The first rap artist to appear on VMA's stage is Run-D.M.C. performing a rap of the VMA "Rules."

PERFORMERS

Pat Benatar	"Seven Rooms of Gloom"
John Cougar Mellencamp	"Lonely Ol' Night"
Eurythmics	"Would I Lie to You?"
Sting	"If You Love Somebody Set Them Free"
Tears for Fears	"Shout"
Daryl Hall and John Oates with Eddie Kendricks and David Ruffin	"The Way You Do the Things You Do"/"My Girl"
Eddie Murphy	"Party All the Time"

WINNERS

Best Video	Don Henley, "The Boys of Summer"
Best Male Video	Bruce Springsteen, "I'm on Fire"
Best Female Video	Tina Turner, "What's Love Got to Do with It"
Best Group Video	USA for Africa, "We Are the World"
Best New Artist	'Til Tuesday, "Voices Carry"
Video Vanguard	David Byrne, Kevin Godley and Lol Creme, Russell Mulcahy
Viewer's Choice	USA for Africa, "We Are the World"

ICE CUBE One of the first videos I dug was "Rock Box." It was off the hook. Run-D.M.C. gettin' busy. I was jealous. As a young kid watching them, you know, yeah—everybody that watched videos want to be on one sooner or later.

JOE DAVOLA, former executive The second year, they needed to get Eddie Murphy as a host. One of the deals that MTV had to do to convince him to do the show was to pay for the video for "Party All the Time." And if you look at the clip, the executive who ran MTV at that time, Les Garland, appears in a scene in a studio control room.

BOB PITTMAN, co-founder Eddie Murphy said, "I don't want a script." And I called Jeff Katzenberg, who had done work with him on motion pictures. So I said, "Gee, I don't know if I wanna do this. What do you think?" He said, "Ah, don't worry. He's really professional." Of course, he gets up onstage and starts talking about fire coming out of his dick. So that was an interesting night.

LES GARLAND, former executive We were losing TV and radio syndication stations left and right. They were unplugging us during the monologue. Pittman comes running toward me, going, "Stop him! Stop him."

"You mean you want me to run onstage and get him?"

I run backstage as he comes off for the first commercial break. He's got that big smile on his face.

"Eddie, what are you doing? You can't say what you're saying on TV."

"You just told me I couldn't say 'shit' and 'fuck.'"

"No, you can't say words like that. You can't say any of those words."

"No, I thought you meant I couldn't say those two."

Nina Blackwood

1981–86

NINA BLACKWOOD I saw this article about MTV
looking for video jockeys...hosts. And I'm like, that's
what I'm doing with these other projects. I got out my
resume and my good old eight-by-tens. I thought, I
have to do something that makes this stand out. I took
a box of crayons and started making it punk-style by
coloring it pink and black and turquoise.

I was a little bit reluctant about moving to New York,
just because my ties were in California. So the
producers took me all over the glamorous parts of
New York. They took me to Tavern on the Green,
where I choked on my bread. Robert Morton had to
give me the Heimlich maneuver. Morton said, "You
owe me. I just saved your life. You have to take the
job." I went, "You're right, that's an omen." I made my
decision right then and there. I thought I'd try it for
three months.

TRL Photo Shoot

CARSON DALY Getting a lot of *TRL* artists who have been on the show consistently—people like Jennifer Lopez, Destiny's Child, Christina, Britney, *NSYNC, Goo Goo Dolls—all people in the same place at the same time is damn near impossible. So we did it around the Grammys® and everybody came to this abandoned hotel.

We put out a wish list of artists that we wanted and it was interesting to see who was willing to check their ego at the door and be a part of this thing. We play the Backstreet Boys next to Limp Bizkit. I go on the air and endorse all of it. I'm not too proud to say this is a good pop song or this is a good rock song or whatever.

Christina and Britney both were there and I didn't see one moment of static. Lenny Kravitz met Fred Durst for the first time that night. And Fred Durst is constantly around controversy but I tip my hat to that guy for the way he acted at that *TRL* photo shoot. He hung out with everybody and was cool. We'll never forget who showed up that day and who was in town. In fact one major, major, major, major, major *TRL* act was two blocks away and couldn't take the time to come down for a picture. And I know who that is and I think it will play a major role at some point in their career. Karma will come back and get them.

ANANDA LEWIS I really like Christina and I don't like what's happened to her now that her career has blown up. I met her before that and she seemed so humble and down to earth. I just thought she would keep that.

Now Christina, this is not personal . . . I was covering the red carpet for the photo shoot. David LaChapelle, one of the greatest photographers in the country, he's doing this shoot. We were in this amazing hallway, I forget where we were shooting, this huge auditorium. There were stairs, red stairs going up. So there were people sitting on the stairs. Limp Bizkit, Goo Goo Dolls, Puffy, Jennifer Lopez, *NSYNC, me, Carson. We're all situated and we walk in and there's all these people painted in gold and they have TVs on their head.

Christina walks in, everybody's already situated. Destiny's Child is there, Lenny Kravitz is there. Britney's on the floor sprawled out, looking gorgeous, I think she has this pretty leather with gold and Christina walks in looking gorgeous, too. She's one of the last people to situate. So David goes, "Everybody's here, where do you want to sit?" She scans the crowd to see where she wants to sit and Britney's right here lying down and Christina went "Uh-uh," shaking her head, and walks to the other side. I don't know her well enough to know her expressions but the energy was, "Puhh. I'm not sitting next to *her*."

FRED DURST The *TRL* photo shoot was great because I was messing with everybody. It was killer, man. I was kicking it with the *NSYNC guys. Those guys are funny. Puffy. Everybody. I got to get some candid stuff from them. They didn't know I was mic'd but Puffy was like, "Man you got a mic on."

It was a pretty cool photo shoot, actually. Britney wouldn't talk to us. But I met Lenny Kravitz that day. Told him what a huge fan I am and how I'd love to work with him and he said the same and I couldn't believe it.

That was also the first time I really got to talk to Christina Aguilera. This crush I've established for Christina, that was a great way for me to talk to her. And it was so cool because I knew she wasn't having it. So I was just pushing it hard, man. I was like, "What's up, good looking?" She was like, "Are you drunk?"

Me and Christina have hung out a couple of times. I'm actually pretty intrigued by her voice. And I think she's really cute and I'd love to hook up with her. I went down to her video shoot to see her. We saw each other in a studio once. And I think the rumors just got around.

Nothing happened. We kissed once. She kisses really good, actually.

BRIAN McFAYDEN I went to the *TRL* photo shoot. It was an ego fest. Everyone was trying to be the cool star of *TRL*. It was like the *TRL* music awards show.

And then you see the Goo Goo Dolls sitting up in the corner just kind of going, "We're the only rock band here besides, you know, Fred Durst from Limp Bizkit.

What the hell are we doing here with all these rappers and R&B singers and boy bands?"

I was kinda hoping somebody would get into a fight, like Christina and Britney.

The photo shoot was taking a long time. There were these naked girls painted gold and everyone was like *wow, this is so cool*. David LaChapelle is just a great photographer, he's got a weird, demented sick mind. He's got these naked chicks, these half-naked dudes, and midgets—little people. He painted them all gold and he had all these artists who have never sat down for longer than ten minutes, and he had all these guys sit there and try and behave and stand up and take their shirts off. He was trying to get Tyrese to take his shirt off. I remember it was over an hour of sitting there before the photo shoot, and there was this little bar area where people were having drinks and whatnot.

I think it was Fred Durst who had to go to the bathroom really bad. The shoot took about two hours and as soon as it was over, the second after Dave said, "That's it," I saw Fred jump up and sprint for the bathroom.

I'm sitting down with *NSYNC, it's the first time I ever met *NSYNC and they come in and they're just kind of like, "We're *NSYNC, you know." I had never worked with boy bands before. And they come in and it was pretty cool to sit down and have a conversation with them. They just could not concentrate on anything I was asking them.

I was just like, "Okay, this is kinda cool, let's just chill with these guys to see what a boy band's actually like." So I'm sitting there and they could not concentrate because Jennifer Lopez just walked in wearing a green dress. So they're trying to flirt with her, they're like looking around, and she sits behind them and they turn around and look at her and she catches them looking at her and they're like little school boys trying to play this game of "1, 2, 3, Jennifer." Like eighth graders do.

Here's *NSYNC, these five guys who every teenage girl desires, and they're trying to get Puffy's girl.

Adam Curry

1987–93

ADAM CURRY I started in radio when I was about fifteen. I grew up in Holland near Amsterdam. I built a transmitter. To see how far it would reach, my mom put me in the car and drove me around. I had a little local radio station, maybe five people listening.

KEVIN SEAL There was a lot of excitement surrounding Adam. From Holland or Belgium or Luxembourg or one of those countries. We were surprised because he was so tall and was paid so much more than the rest of us. Back in Luxembourg, he was a big star. But he was a very humble man. I was bringing him his laundry and he opened the door himself. He had just taken a shower and his hair was all ratted and hanging down. He said, "Thanks Kev." He was not a big tipper. It's not in his culture over there.

ADAM CURRY My first assignment was on Halloween. I came dressed as a gangster. Imagine walking into a room with Downtown Julie Brown and Kevin Seal and Carolyne Heldman and they're all dressed up in costume. They're weird without a costume. You could already see some of the dynamics that were going on. Immediately I knew that Julie Brown was going to be interesting, and Kevin off his rocker, and Goodman was just on his way out. It was an interesting introduction to everybody.

KEVIN SEAL That's his real hair. Once when he wasn't looking, I checked. Even if it is a good weave, you can always see it, especially with blond hair like that. That's his own hair. You're not allowed but I did. I got a pair of medical forceps and gave it a good yank. It's his. It's impressive when you think about it. A lot of people don't have their real hair. Marv Albert comes to mind.

ADAM CURRY My shtick was hair. Definitely had hair. Some European vibe going on. I think I pissed everybody off from day one. Certainly the PR department. The first day I was in, I was doing an interview with *TV Guide* and I told them, "Yeah I know Madonna and she's not necessarily the sweetest girl in the world." She couldn't believe that I had said something like that. It all went downhill from there.

DAISY FUENTES We both lived in New Jersey. I was driving this crummy Pontiac Fiero and he was driving this big green Rolls-Royce. I just saw the big hair, and I pulled up next to him and honked the horn. He was trying to ignore me but we were stuck in bumper-to-bumper traffic. I told him to roll down the window and asked if he had any Grey Poupon. He leans over to his glove compartment and pulls out a Grey Poupon. I thought, "He's retarded."

YOU MUST BE THIS TA

Moscow Peace and Music Festival

ADAM CURRY That was a major party from beginning to end. We were essentially going to create this concert at Lenin Stadium in Moscow. It was Bon Jovi and Mötley Crüe, Ozzy, Skid Row, Cinderella. That was a trip, flying for eighteen hours; basically, the whole plane was coach. It was not like this luxury jet. I was in the back with Tico Torres [of Bon Jovi] and his then girlfriend and we were playing some name-that-band game or whatever. Of course there were no drugs and no booze allowed because this was the let's-rock-against-drugs-and-alcohol show but I had the feeling that something might have slipped on board, particularly when Ozzy was pacing around the toilet. He had to go to the bathroom and was just out of his mind. On what I don't know but he was out of his mind and Sharon was in the back and all of a sudden, it was like, "Man, Ozzy just pissed in his pants!" And his whole crotch is just completely wet and he's like, "Oh I couldn't wait anymore!" and he just went back and sat and fell back asleep and that was it.

We picked up the Scorpions in Germany and when those guys got on the plane, they were really, really out of control. Sebastian Bach and Zakk Wylde, they were into this thing of, "Hey let's put a cigarette out on our hand and see if we can let it burn all the way up." That was 100 percent rock 'n' roll.

PATRICK BYRNES, producer I remember being halfway around the world and exhausted. Our first meal was a shock and we all went to the hotel hungry. Laid on the lumpiest bed in history. In the dim light as my head hit the pillow, I realized that the movement at the foot of my bed was roaches. Running over the sheets—everywhere. Got no sleep. Next morning, I tried the showers . . . only to find no curtain and no water pressure. All the Americans or English-speaking people totally bonded. We soon ended up eating all our meals at catering over at the stadium with Mötley Crüe, Bon Jovi, Ozzy, and Skid Row. Everyone was so warm and friendly. I remember traveling with Ozzy on a bus and having him excuse himself to go pee. Except there wasn't a bathroom. He whipped it out and peed on the floor by the back door.

ADAM CURRY The show was great. It was strange. Here are these kids who have never been exposed to bands like Crüe and Bon Jovi, and at the same time there was a lot of tension going on between Bon Jovi and Mötley Crüe because no one was supposed to be a headliner. But Ozzy stole the show. The kids knew Ozzy. I don't know how but they knew every single song. They went nuts. They were just spitting into the air. That's how excited they were.

VMA 1986

DATE September 6
LOCATIONS The Palladium, New York; and Universal Amphitheatre, Los Angeles
HOST Multiple presenters

PERFORMERS

Genesis	"Throwin' It All Away"
The Hooters	"And We Danced" / "Nervous Night"
Whitney Houston	"How Will I Know?"/ "The Greatest Love of All"
INXS	"What You Need"
Mr. Mister	"Kyrie"/"Broken Wings"
The Monkees	"I'm a Believer"/"Daydream Believer"
Robert Palmer	"Addicted to Love"
Pet Shop Boys	"Love Comes Quickly"/"West End Girls"
Simply Red	"Holding Back the Years"/ "Money's Too Tight to Mention"
'Til Tuesday	"What About Love?"
Tina Turner	"Typical Male"
Van Halen	"Best of Both Worlds"/ "Love Comes Walkin' In"

WINNERS

Best Video	Dire Straits, "Money for Nothing"
Best Male Video	Robert Palmer, "Addicted to Love"
Best Female Video	Whitney Houston, "How Will I Know?"
Best Group Video	Dire Straits, "Money for Nothing"
Best New Artist	a-ha, "Take on Me"
Video Vanguard	Madonna and Zbigniew Rybczynski
Viewer's Choice	a-ha, "Take on Me"

KURT LODER I didn't even have cable at that time. Among people who were making their living in print, as I was, everyone looked down on the Video Music Awards. Just the idea. Video first, music second. Says it all. Obviously, Satan had taken over the world. No one could ever take this seriously. And yet, when you go to the Video Music Awards, it's more like rock 'n' roll has traditionally been than any other function. The real rock 'n' roll lifestyle, I think, is people staying up late, and smoking and drinking, and doing things they regret the next day, and that happens every year. They're keeping a tradition alive here. I was wrong when I thought otherwise. I'm sorry.

Free Your Mind

Enough Is Enough

MTV's 1993 "Free Your Mind" campaign focused on racial mistrust, homophobia, sexism, and religious intolerance, and looked at the role music plays in either dispelling or perpetuating people's fears. Among the MTV News special reports were "Straight from the Hood," a look at young people growing up in South Central Los Angeles after the 1992 riots; and "Hate Rock," which examined "Oi!" music and its link to a growing global neo-Nazi movement promoting racial hatred and violence. MTV's "Free Your Mind Forum"—moderated by Tabitha Soren and Alison Stewart—explored racial, sexual, and religious intolerance in America with a live studio audience.

World AIDS Day

As the first network to broadcast a public service announcement advocating condom use, MTV is committed to keeping its viewers informed about AIDS. Each December 1 since 1996, MTV has commemorated World Aids Day with a series of specials featuring reportage from MTV bureaus around the globe. "Positively Global," "Staying Alive," and "True Life: This Could Be You" are among the programs that have examined the impact of the disease on young people in Asia, Europe, Latin America, and the United States.

The Scroll

STEPHEN FRIEDMAN We were talking about launching the antidiscrimination campaign to coincide with the *Matthew Shepard Story: Anatomy of a Hate Crime*. That's specifically about discrimination against gays and lesbians, but we wanted to tell the audience that these hate crimes happen every day to all kinds of people, young and old. And our feeling was "What better way to do it than to do the scroll for hours and hours after we do this movie?" What staggered us is that so many young people read that those words can lead to violence.

A series of reports designed to raise young people's awareness of the tragic consequences of violence, the 1994 "Enough Is Enough" campaign included a forum where President Clinton spoke with a group of two hundred young people between the ages of sixteen and twenty, attempting to answer their questions about the growing problem of violence in society.

Remote Control

PREMIERE December 7, 1987

JOE DAVOLA, cocreator and producer MTV was moving into the second phase—doing stripped programming. Half-hour shows other than videos. They pulled three producers from the producing pool. Rene Garcia, Linda Corradina, and me. Rene was to do a dance show, which became *Club MTV.* Linda did *The Week in Rock.* I was told to do a game show.

I was really against doing it. It was taking me away from the road, working with rock stars, enjoying what I was doing. Fortunately it turned out to be something good. They put me together with a writer named Mike Dugan and they said to come up with a show. We took a hotel room, and we just started talking about what would be a good MTV show. We started talking about trivia and about how kids grew up on those old TV shows. We felt that's the thing that we wanted to do. Hence, we came up with *Remote Control.*

KEN OBER We did five trial shows. I remember watching them with Colin and going, "Oh, my Lord. We are screwed. We have made the biggest mistake."

COLIN QUINN So we were like, "Oh man, I hope they don't see this show." Even then in the clubs, a Brady Bunch joke was a hack to us. So I did all these Brady Bunch things, thinking thank God no one's going to see this show. But then, all the comedians were like, "No, the show's hilarious."

DENIS LEARY Well it was just a lot of fun because we all knew each other and it was kind of insane. We did three or four tapings per day for a few months at a time. We went to work every day at six o'clock in the morning. You had me, Quinn, Sandler, Stiller—all the writers who were fucking nuts anyways. We had one boom box. We'd have arguments over who was gonna play what. So every day was fun. It was just kind of everybody busting each other's balls. My most cognizant memory of that show is when Colin and I used to have these fake fights. And I can't remember if I fucking drew blood from him or if he drew blood from me or maybe we did both on various days, but I do remember that there was blood and people thought it was a gag.

KEN OBER Having since worked on other game shows, I've come to realize now just how special the whole experience was, that we were free to do

whatever we wanted. I mean, you had to play the game. There were rules. But we were free to do anything. And, if you had an idea during the taping of the show, you just went with it.

There was one show where the contestants just flat out sucked. All of them, they were the stupidest people you could *ever* find, let alone find in a game show. And none of them had any points after the first or second round. I said something like, "We should just throw you off the game and pick three random people off the street." Joe Davola was in my earpiece and he just went, "Go ahead, throw them off the air."

We threw these people off the air and picked three people out of the audience and played the rest of the game.

DENIS LEARY The scripts would only exist in the sense of asking the questions. Everything else was really off the cuff. So off the cuff that Sandler's shit used to make us all look at each other and go, "Why is everybody fucking laughing? We don't get it." He'd just come out and basically he'd be in a bathing suit or he'd be in some ridiculous fucking outfit. And, you know, never do the script. Just kind of stand there

and start making shit up. So there was a lot of that, where he'd just come and do whatever the fuck he wanted to do. And then the script was whatever question Kenny had to ask the contestants, you know?

KEN OBER There's entertainment value in the categories—that started with *Remote Control.* I was always amazed at how prolific the writers were in coming up with these wild categories. There was one that started off as "Dead or Alive." They would say a name and you'd have to say if the person was dead or alive. Then the next week that category became "Dead or Canadian." Then it was Dead, Alive, or Indian Food.

People had to lie in the Craftmatic Adjustable Bed and watch videos. Which became like the center of all sex activity after hours, I found out. I never got involved in it. But there were rumors that was the thing to do, to have sex on the Craftmatic Adjustable when the studio was down. Many members of the crew took advantage of that. My relationship with the Craftmatic was purely professional all the way.

Ken Ober

1987–90

KEN OBER I was in New York as a stand-up comedian, going to clubs. Going out for commercials and stupid TV pilots like everybody else at the time. I got sent up for the *Remote Control* job. I remember not being interested because it just sounded goofy. My agent at the time said it wouldn't hurt. "

That started the process rolling of audition after audition after audition. I was going to Hawaii for a couple of weeks with a friend of mine, and they couldn't make their mind up. It was between me and Danny Bonaduce. Danny Partridge or this unknown guy? I check into my hotel in Hawaii, boom, there's a message on the phone. "Get back to New York."

What scared me was that I was just starting out in my career. I'm going to be a game show host? At that time, MTV hadn't had any regular shows on. MTV was primarily a music network. That's all they did. So being on a game show on MTV at that time just sounded like, "Well, I don't know if I want to flush my career down the toilet before it's even started."

Adam Sandler

1989–90

KEN OBER Colin Quinn was good friends with Sandler and was always pushing MTV to use him on the show. Sandler was so young. He was a little kid.

COLIN QUINN What ever happened to him?

DOUG HERZOG, former executive I remember meeting Adam. I went to see the woman who used to host that USA show *Up All Night*, Rhonda Shear, at the Comic Strip. This kid, Adam Sandler, is one of the opening acts, and he gets on stage, and he just completely charmed me. He was still at NYU, didn't have much of an act.

I followed him out into the bar after his set, and said, 'I'm from MTV. I think you're really funny, and I think we should put you on *Remote Control*." He was like, "Wow, cool." I called *Remote Control* and said, "I'm going to send this kid Adam down. You guys should figure out something." They all said, "Who's he? We don't want to do anything with him."

COLIN QUINN They said, "Okay you're going to be Bossy Boy," some new character they thought up. They just put this horrible orange wig on him, and took a Magic Marker and gave him freckles, and put on a Burger King uniform. Even *he* didn't know what the hell he was doing. Ken Ober would just start yelling in the middle of the show, "Yeah, great character, Adam."

JOE DAVOLA Adam was still going to school at NYU and we were going over to the dorm and partying with him and having keg parties on Friday nights. It was amazing. This guy was a sophomore or junior and we were having him on MTV.

CHRIS KRESKI, writer I don't think he was even in his twenties. The dumber idea you gave him, the funnier he'd be with it. We turned him into the Stud Boy, this highly inappropriate paid escort for older Hollywood actresses. He would go into great detail about their date and what would go on between them. He was so funny at it that we just kept giving him characters and making him "something Boy." He was Pool Boy and Boston Boy and Hot Dog Boy.

KEN OBER You would suggest some character to him and, boom, it would go into Adam's brain, he would come out with a new character. He was a real integral part of the show. It really is amazing. From Stud Boy to Twenty-Million-Dollars-a-Film Boy.

Colin Quinn

1989–90

COLIN QUINN I started doing stand-up comedy. MTV started showing up at the clubs. I ended up doing this little MTV comedy special. The minute we did the special, I looked at my check and said, "Boy, these guys don't pay very well. Good thing I don't work for them full-time." Little did I know. That was the biggest check I ever got from them.

DOUG HERZOG Michael Dugan, who cocreated *Remote Control* with Joe Davola, had the idea of bringing Colin in as the announcer. I thought it was a terrible idea. He doesn't have an announcer's voice.

JOE DAVOLA Because we were MTV we wanted someone who was against what real TV announcers are. So we wanted to get somebody who didn't enunciate correctly and also had a harsh voice.

COLIN QUINN When I first got the job, I was arrogant. They gave me this prize copy to read. I had just done a commercial so I thought I knew the commercial industry. I had gotten like four thousand bucks for this Burger King commercial. They handed me all this prize copy, I was thinking to myself, "Boy, you must get a lot of money for this." I go, "How much do I get for this?" They go, "Nothing. It's part of the job." *What?*

At the audition, I was mispronouncing all the things. I'd be reading this copy, sneering. Doug Herzog goes, "That snotty bastard, we should fire him. I don't want him around here anymore." He was going to fire me at the audition.

Then we made it into a thing where it became deliberate mispronunciations. They would always complain, but MTV liked it. All the advertisers would go, "Hey, they're mispronouncing our products. They're making fun of them." But it just worked on the show.

KEN OBER Colin would smoke while he was reading the copy. If he had an on-camera read, he'd have a cigarette in his hand. It was just hysterical to watch.

He really hated doing it. One time he made fun of American Airlines. "American Airlines, it flies to fifteen destinations. Destinations that you wouldn't want to be in even if you're in the witness protection program." We get this call and they pulled out as the sponsor.

Eventually, they made Kari Wuhrer start doing them.

COLIN QUINN Off camera, my only move to make people laugh was to take out my penis. Nowadays it sounds like sexual harassment. But it really wasn't, and that's not denigrating my penis. We would walk around the office and just start talking to you and they go, "Oh, my God." I started doing it on the show, behind the counter. Kari would say, "When *Remote Control* continues . . ." And then she'd notice and say, "When *Remote Control* oh my God!" We were always semiexposed around the place. I wasn't the only one. But I was the major one.

KEN OBER Everyone was always taking their penises out on *Remote Control*. You have to remember, it was in the late '80s, early '90s. It was a very free time. We weren't living under the umbrella of sexual harassment and political correctness that we are now. Men were more free to take their penises out. Crew guy's penises might be out, one of the writers would come down, stand there with his penis out. You would just never know whose penis would be out at any given time.

COLIN QUINN We had a big dinner at some Spanish restaurant. They brought out a tiramisu. I took it under the table and put an imprint of my penis in the tiramisu. And then put it back on the table. And everybody's like, "Oh my God!"

Denis Leary

TED DEMME In 1990, I had seen Denis's stand-up routine, *No Cure for Cancer*, off-Broadway, and it literally was the smartest, coolest, funniest thing I'd ever seen in my life. I met with him afterward. Denis and I took his show and turned it into thirty-second bits. We would go out and shoot for a Saturday and Sunday, about forty spots. I didn't know how to cut them. Some of them were just jump-cut by accident. It looked so exciting. I'd like to think that I just created something on purpose, but I didn't. It was just a "Oh wow that kind of looks cool" mistake.

They didn't quite know what would happen with Denis once they aired them. They sensed that he would just go through the roof, and he did, as soon as those things aired. Every commercial break, they were on. It was catching fire in a bottle.

DENIS LEARY Some of the stuff was from the show, but most of it was stuff that I specifically designed for Teddy. And then there was other stuff that Teddy would shout from behind the camera while we were shooting stuff that he heard me say when were having dinner and having drinks. He would just yell it out. And, because he knew he was gonna edit in this very choppy way, it didn't matter. There was no continuity. So he really deserves the credit for the spot. He basically made my career happen.

TED DEMME I knew Denis had hit a total peak when, one day in my office, a messenger came in with a box of Eskimo Pies and it said, "Love, Richard" on it. I remembered the Cindy Crawford spot we did, where the last thing Denis says is, "I want to see Cindy everywhere, I want to see Cindy on top of the Empire State Building naked eating a box of Eskimo Pies." So Richard Gere sent this box of Eskimo Pies: "To Ted and Denis, Love, Richard."

COLIN QUINN Denis came the last two seasons of *Remote Control*.

CHRIS KRESKI Quinn knew him from Boston and brought him in. Everything we did with Leary was created to make fun of Colin.

KEN OBER When he played Keith Richards, he would come out and ask music questions. And he looked just like Keith. He did another guy named Stickpin Quinn, who is Colin's stepbrother. They would come out and they would start to fight. But they would start to *really* fight. They would really punch and kick each other.

COLIN QUINN A couple of times I got hurt. We were just rolling around on the floor kicking each other. Then Ken Ober would make an IRA joke to make us stop fighting, 'cause that's how we always ended it.

KEN OBER I think Leary broke or bruised Quinn's ribs once. There would be bloody noses. It's unbelievable.

VMA 1992

DATE September 9
LOCATION UCLA's Pauley Pavilion, Los Angeles
HOST Dana Carvey

PERFORMERS

Bryan Adams	"Do I Have to Say the Words"
Eric Clapton	"Tears in Heaven"
The Black Crowes	"Remedy"
Bobby Brown	"Humpin' Around"
Def Leppard	"Let's Get Rocked"
En Vogue	"Free Your Mind"
Guns N' Roses with Elton John	"November Rain"
Michael Jackson	"Black or White"
Elton John	"The One"
Nirvana	"Lithium"
Pearl Jam	"Jeremy"
Red Hot Chili Peppers	"Give It Away"
U2	"Even Better Than the Real Thing"

WINNERS

Best Video	Van Halen, "Right Now"
Best Male Video	Eric Clapton, "Tears in Heaven"
Best Female Video	Annie Lennox, "Why"
Best Group Video	U2, "Even Better Than the Real Thing"
Best Rap Video	Arrested Development, "Tennessee"
Best Dance Video	Prince and the New Power Generation, "Cream"
Best Metal/ Hard Rock Video	Metallica, "Enter Sandman"
Best Alternative Music Video	Nirvana, "Smells Like Teen Spirit"
Best New Artist	Nirvana, "Smells Like Teen Spirit"
Breakthrough Video	Red Hot Chili Peppers, "Give It Away"
Michael Jackson's Video Vanguard	Guns N' Roses
Viewer's Choice	Red Hot Chili Peppers, "Under the Bridge"

KURT LODER "Rape Me" was a new song that Kurt Cobain had whipped up, and he showed up at the Video Music Awards and says, "Instead of doing the hit you've brought me here to play, I would like to do 'Rape Me.'" And they're going, "No. Do a song called 'Rape Me'? That would be bad."

JOEL GALLEN When Nirvana's turn finally came about halfway through the show, Kurt Cobain decided to have some fun. They were supposed to play "Lithium." But first they played the first few chords of "Rape Me," they did about four bars of it, and then went right into "Lithium."

KURT LODER When he started strumming the opening chords to "Rape Me," going "Rape me, da, da, da . . ." I'm sure fifty suits in the back fell right over.

DOUG HERZOG We all went, "Huh?!" That was the exact reaction they were looking for, and they got it. You had to appreciate the fact that they tweaked us a little bit. We were in the truck, going, "Huh?!" And then we're like, "Ooooh." They're going, "Gotcha!"

JOEL GALLEN Halfway through the song, people started getting up onstage and stage-diving. One of the VJs did it, too—Steve Isaacs. At the end Nirvana's bass player, in jubilation, throws his bass way in the air and tries to catch it. But it hits him in the head and almost knocks him out. Then Kurt throws his guitar through the bass equipment. And Dave is bashing all the drums. They start knocking the amps over. Then Dave runs to the mike and starts yelling Axl's name. Guns N' Roses had some words with them and Dave is yelling. "Axl, where's Axl?"

TABITHA SOREN Backstage at the Pauley Pavilion, trailers were all lined up right next to each other. Anybody who wanted more space than just their trailer had to go outside. Which forced a lot of people together who, normally, probably wouldn't have had anything to do with each other.

Two of the bands who were there were Guns N' Roses and Nirvana. Both of them at the prime height of their popularity, and their egos clashed. As Axl's walking down the grass, he saw Courtney and Kurt. Courtney said something to him, but Axl ended up looking at Kurt and saying, "Hey, control your woman." Actually, something a little more derogatory than that. Kurt and Courtney just looked at him and burst out laughing. It certainly made the Video Music Awards much more exciting that year, because there was this tension backstage. There was a sort of a rivalry between the two camps, alternative rock going head-to-head with the veterans of heavy metal.

SLASH I was like, "I don't have time for this shit." Duff told me, I think, he got into a fight with their bass player, and Axl got into a fight with Kurt and I was like, "Yeah, yeah, yeah." It didn't really have any significance as far as going up there and actually playing. And as far as the bands were concerned, "I'm in this band, you're in that band, never should the twain meet on the same ground." Simple as that. So I wasn't a part of that. There's no need for arguing unless it's a direct confrontation.

JOEL GALLEN Howard Stern said that he wouldn't do the show unless he could come on as Fartman. Howard wasn't nearly as popular then as he is now. I had to do some convincing and selling on this. To have him come on as Fartman, and farting on the air, hey, we're MTV, but there are certain points where you draw the line.

He was going to fly in and meet another presenter at the podium. He had this list of people that he was sure would do it with him. We went through the list. Drew Barrymore and about half a dozen other people were like, "What are you, crazy? We're not gonna do that! We don't want to copresent with Fartman!"

KURT LODER I wish the movie had happened. Howard Stern—genius. I wish he could be a part of the Video Music Awards every year. Coming down on the wire, in the suit, blowing over a desk or something with his Fartman act. How offensive was that? That was just great. We could use more of that.

JOEL GALLEN Finally we got Luke Perry to do it. He totally had a good sense of humor about the whole thing. Howard flies in to do his bit. We had a special-effects podium so he was able to fart at it and of course the podium blew up.

When he was about to leave, he was supposed to get flown off. But he started walking off. All of a sudden, the guy hit the button for him to start flying out, and he starts to get tangled in the wires.

It made a big impact on Howard's life. If you saw the Howard Stern movie, he re-created that scene to open it.

ALISON STEWART, producer Howard Stern came into the interview tent dressed as Fartman, and he wouldn't leave the tent until I touched his butt. *He would not leave.* It was my first big thing and Peter Gabriel and Sting were stacking up outside the tent and they were going to walk away. He would not leave and in the line of duty I had to touch Howard Stern's butt. That was before he started working out, too!

LARS ULRICH I know it meant a lot to Axl. One of Axl's big heroes is Elton John and for him to do that song with Elton—he told me that "November Rain" was his ode to all those great Elton John ballads—that was pretty cool.

Fab Five Freddy

1988–92

TED DEMME Fab Five Freddy is probably the coolest man alive. Back in 1988, he was an underground hip-hop connoisseur. He knew everything. He was an amazing graffiti artist. He was mentioned in the Blondie song "Rapture." He was just this really cool, downtown New York guy who always wore a hat, always wore glasses, always wore the coolest duds. Peter Dougherty had known him from the underground hip-hop scene. Fab had never done anything on camera, and I had never directed anyone on camera. So it was a perfect marriage of two guys that had no experience, no business doing anything like we were doing, but pulling it off. Fab is an icon and he always will be. Every kid that came on our show wanted to be on with Fab Five Freddy because Fab kind of validated you on the show. That meant not only were you down but you're probably selling some records, too.

ICE-T Freddy was a very powerful force in hip-hop. You know, being a spokesperson, being on *Yo! MTV Raps*, and knowing everybody in hip-hop at the time, and being a graffiti writer. He was deeply embedded into the scene. Actually, Freddy made one of the most famous hip-hop records of all time, "Change of the Beat," which any time you've ever heard anybody scratch "fresh," that's Freddy's voice.

yo! mtv raps today
FIRST SHOW

Ed Lover and Dr. Dre

1989–95

CHUCK D The fact that Ed Lover and Dre were on every day was as monumental as Dick Clark when he did *American Bandstand* back in the late '50s. Everything they did every day was hilarious.

TED DEMME, co-creator and producer I had actually grown up with Ed through a number of places in the Queens/Long Island area. Once *Yo! MTV Raps* had hit, Ed called me up every week. "Hey man, you gotta put me on." I'm like, "Ed, I'm lucky to have a job, I can't just put my friends on the show. What are you—nuts?" At the same time, this guy Dr. Dre would be calling me up, making me laugh on the phone. I checked out the guy and he's the Beastie Boys' DJ. He's a big, cheery round guy with a great sense of humor, really funny.

Fab Five Freddy's *Yo! MTV Raps* show, weekly, was hitting all these ratings. They said, "OK, we want to put it on every day. Get some more hosts for Monday through Friday and it has to be on in three days." So I call up Ed, I call up Dre. I go, "Meet me in the park in a half hour." I brought a camera. I introduced them to each other. I go, "All right, I want you to say, 'Welcome back to *Yo! MTV Raps*,' you say who you are, talk a little bit about this Public Enemy video we're gonna show, make me laugh a little bit, and then lead to the video."

The first time they did it, it was like they'd been doing it forever. From the first day they came on the show, they were getting so many letters, 'cause they were on in the afternoon when kids were watching. Back then a lot of the rap videos were really hard. NWA, Eric B., a lot of those videos couldn't be shown during the week. Ed and Dre brought a sense of humor to what we were doing.

That first year we went to spring break and MTV invited us to go down and do a lot of the programming down there. Ed and Dre would just get mobbed everywhere they went. We were all, collectively at MTV, like, "What have we created here? What is going on?"

ED LOVER Dre and I were both vying at the same time but we didn't know each other, for *Yo! MTV Raps Today*, which was the daily show because Fab Five Freddy at the time didn't want to overexpose himself by doing it five . . .

DR. DRE That was a great reason. He was a beautiful man. Any man that would pass up a chance and let these two shleps come on and make it happen . . . I gotta thank you for that, Five.

ED LOVER That's how we got our role. We shared one paycheck, they didn't really have any money. So we split the money and we didn't have a dressing room . . .

DR. DRE Split that, too.

ED LOVER We used to dress on the set and we used to just do everything, it was just like a little corner of the actual studio that we used to crank out *Yo! MTV Raps* from.

DR. DRE And we'd use everything on the set to improvise to make the show with. Fab would go out to locations and do his show live from there. We would do everything from inside the studio—

ED LOVER —Until we decided we wanted to go on the road and then they said, "Do it on the blue screen." So the road is moving behind us and we're on a bike and a Yo bus. Just introducing videos would have been boring so we started coming up with stuff that would happen spontaneously on the set.

DR. DRE Our comic nature took over. It just kind of naturally regressed to, "Hey, guess what I thought of . . ." And I'd come up with a character like the Nubian-nator and Burnt Man and Aunt Floyd. The funniest character was Burnt Man, a takeoff on the *Dark Man* movie. His evolution came from him being stuck in a back room and he got caught on fire. And then we made up the Real Michael Jackson, who was kidnapped when Mike was seven years old.

MISSY ELLIOT They were just always wilding out. They crossed all boundaries, every day they did something crazy. All I knew was they kept me laughing. I used to wig out on *Yo! MTV Raps*.

Yo! MTV Raps

PREMIERE August 6, 1988

CHUCK D I was part of the first *Yo! MTV Raps* pilot in 1988. We played in a barn as a part of the Run's House tour. And this was Austin, Texas. It was Run-D.M.C., Jazzy Jeff and the Fresh Prince, EPMD, JJ Fad, and Public Enemy. And we saw Ted Demme and his crew come backstage and say they were going to put together a rap show for MTV. We said, "It's about time."

TED DEMME It was 1988, and *Club MTV* and *Remote Control* had already been on MTV and found success with the half-hour format. I was always kind of a hip-hop fan, growing up in New York, and I just thought there was a lack of hip-hop music on the channel.

So I went to my boss at the time, Peter Dougherty, who was great friends with Rick Rubin, and was very close with the Beastie Boys. I said, "Let's do a hip-hop show. Let's do an hour special, at least, that can air whenever. We can do the ten best rap videos, we'll do some interviews. We'll do some packages."

After trying to keep pitching it to our boss, they finally said "All right, why don't you go do it."

ICE CUBE Now we had a national show dedicated to our music. So it was real exciting to me and I couldn't wait to see next week. It was coming on every day when it first came on and it was right up my alley.

TED DEMME Run-D.M.C. was really the only group that was doing anything on MTV. We went to Austin, Texas, in the summer of '88 and we got Run-D.M.C. to be our hosts.

PETER DOUGHERTY, co-creator We went to the gig and shot Run-D.M.C. in this horrible cowshed. Apparently they wouldn't let that kind of music into the "proper" stadium.

SNOOP DOGG It put us on the same page as rock 'n' roll and music in general. And for them to give us our own show with somebody like Fab Five, who would really go find the real hip-hop hits, that was cool, 'cause he started from the beginning in hip-hop, so he knew exactly what hip-hop should be. I remember my first time on *Yo! MTV Raps*, I didn't even look in the camera. I had my head down the whole interview and was real shy. When *Yo!* was around, it was a place where everybody could come, unite, everybody wanted to come on there and showcase their new videos. You could be you, Fab Five was real. That feeling was a beautiful thing and when it disappeared,

we really had no way of communicating with each other. . . as far as hip-hop artists in general.

EMINEM When *Yo! MTV Raps* first came out, I was in my early teens and waiting for something like that to come out. When it did, I was like, "This is dope!" because it gave me and my friends a chance to see the artists that we were buying. What they look like. Their style of dress. The way they move, the way they act.

ED LOVER *Yo! MTV Raps* was responsible for bringing hip-hop to the masses. If you were from Compton, California, you could understand what was going on in New York via hip-hop and vice versa. We would go interview the late great Eazy E and Tupac Shakur and Biggie and show their videos and we'd go to where they came from and where they lived and shoot shows with them.

DR. DRE When we'd do those weeks you'd go to Snoop's house and you'd go to Dre's house, and you'd be there and people would get to see them at home, just being themselves, and people became more in touch with them. They always felt very comfortable with us. The funny thing is, they would always tell us about the crazy stuff that we did in the studio and they would go, "Man I never believe y'all guys do that, y'all are nuts."

EVE *Yo! MTV Raps* was good for the hip-hop world, period. They pretty much played everyone that was out there. It definitely helped hip-hop.

DA BRAT I think the first time I saw MTV I was in junior high school and I saw Fab Five Freddy. I think it was a *Yo!* show. And was it Kool Moe Dee or L.L.? Somebody was on it and it was just totally cute to me. I think it was L.L. And I couldn't watch a lot of rap music at all 'cause I was going to church a lot and my grandmother was sanctified so I kind of had to sneak out and watch it. When I saw that I knew that's where I belonged.

ED LOVER We interviewed Carole King. She was one of our very early guests when we didn't even have any guests on *Yo! MTV Raps*. It was just me and Dre and two stools and a backdrop and a little basketball court that we took out of Ted's office and brought down to the set and Carole King was one of the people we interviewed on *Yo! MTV Raps*.

DR. DRE Uh-huh.

ED LOVER We got flagged from executives 'cause of that. "Why did I turn on my TV, Ed and Dre, and see Carole King?" 'Cause she was on the set gettin' interviewed by somebody else! So we dragged her over and grilled her about her knowledge of hip-hop and, what do you know, she knew nothing.

DR. DRE So it was good.

ED LOVER What did we do? We sang Carole King songs. On *Yo! MTV Raps*.

DR. DRE Who would have known that Lauryn Hill would have been watching that show and been influenced to have the Fugees sing a Carole King song? Who would've known that?

ED LOVER Not me.

DR. DRE Not me.

JA RULE The last show for *Yo! MTV Raps* was hot because you had so many different artists come on and perform their own little thing. Rakim was there. It was really special because it was the end. Whoever was in hip-hop at the time, whoever was historical in hip-hop, they had them all there and everybody had a chance to say good-bye to a monumental show. To me, that was the best episode ever. Even though it was good-bye, it spelled hip-hop all the way.

NELLY

What song best describes your current state of mind?	"So Fresh, So Clean"
What is favorite video of all time?	Dre and Snoop, "G. thang"
What is your first memory of MTV?	*Yo! MTV Raps*
Where were you the first time you saw yourself on MTV and how did you react?	In my crib—very excited—called the rest of the crew to tell them to watch.
Does the video enhance or hinder the song?	———
What is the most memorable moment you've witnessed on MTV?	Halftime (Super Bowl)
Whose video work do you most admire?	———
What do you like most about MTV?	Videos!
What do you like least about MTV?	Some of the videos.
What is your favorite guilty pleasure video?	
What do you consider to be MTV's greatest achievement and/or greatest failure in its first 20 years?	Expansion from not just music, into news, culture, politics, lifestyles, etc. People can look to MTV for a lot, not just videos. Also, it's a forum for all types of artists to express themselves.
What is the worst reaction you've received to one of your videos?	———
Videos should...	———
The best band name	———
The greatest moment in rock and pop and rap was	———
My biggest influence	L.L. Cool J, Michael Jackson
My favorite VMA performance	Besides my own, Janet Jackson! (VMA 2000)
If I were President of MTV I would...	———
What artist would you most like to work with and what would you like to do with them?	C-Lo & Nate Dogg—collaborate on a song & video
Did video kill the radio star?	Video helped the radio star—now you can have images when you're listening to your favorite artist on the radio.

MISSY ELLIOT They still had their shell tops on and that's what kept it gangster 'cause they was like, they didn't get dressed up, it was still Run-D.M.C. and it was still Aerosmith, so it was cool.

VMA 1987

DATE September 11
LOCATION Universal Amphitheatre, Los Angeles
HOST Multiple presenters

Run-D.M.C. performs with Aerosmith onstage at VMAs for a Rap Milestone performance that revives Aerosmith's career.

PERFORMERS

Run-D.M.C. with Steven Tyler and Joe Perry	"Walk This Way"
Bryan Adams	"Victim of Love"/"Only the Strong Survive"
The Bangles	"Walk Like an Egyptian"/ "Walking Down Your Street"
Bon Jovi	"Livin' On a Prayer"
David Bowie	"Never Let Me Down"
The Cars	"You Are the Girl"/"Double Trouble"
Crowded House	"Don't Dream It's Over"/ "Now We're Getting Somewhere"
Whitney Houston	"I Wanna Dance with Somebody"/"Didn't We Almost Have It All"
Cyndi Lauper	"Change of Heart"/"True Colors"
Los Lobos	"La Bamba"
Madonna	"Causing a Commotion"
Prince	"Sign o' the Times"/"Play in the Sunshine"
Whitesnake	"Still of the Night"

WINNERS

Best Video	Peter Gabriel, "Sledgehammer"
Best Male Video	Peter Gabriel, "Sledgehammer"
Best New Artist	Crowded House, "Don't Dream It's Over"
Best Female Video	Madonna, "Papa Don't Preach"
Video Vanguard	Julien Temple and Peter Gabriel
Viewer's Choice	U2, "With or Without You"

Kevin Seal

1987—91

STEVE LEEDS, talent executive We went around to ten universities over two weeks across the country looking for the next VJ as a publicity stunt. We thought we might get lucky and find someone. Kevin Seal's roommate was the one who really wanted to be a VJ. Kevin was just going along for the ride as a dare.

KEVIN SEAL I was bumming around, studying mechanical engineering at the University of Washington in Seattle, my hometown. I was also drinking a lot of high-priced beer. We used to get it for two dollars and fifty cents a case. Not that I recommend that kind of behavior, especially for young people. I've learned my lesson. I had a thirty-seven-inch waist at one point and thought, "That is not attractive on a twenty-four-year-old," let me tell you.

I didn't have cable. I didn't really like rock 'n' roll. The funny thing is, rock 'n' roll didn't really catch on in Seattle until the whole grunge thing happened.

DAISY FUENTES He's just nuts. I think he was missing a chromosome. But what a funny, talented guy.

KEVIN SEAL People actually had to watch the videos for me and tell me what they were like and then go from there. One producer told me for several months that Duran Duran was an all-girl group and they performed nude. Hence the "Girls on Film" video. I introduced that video several times, I believe. But nobody ever called me on it. I don't think that anyone was paying that much attention to it. I was on late at night back then.

JOE PEROTA, director We used to send VJs their scripts by messenger, every night. When faxes just started to come into widespread use, we were going to hook up all the VJs with faxes. Kevin never seemed to get his scripts. No one could figure out why. So once I was at Kevin's house, and I was walking through his living room or whatever and I noticed his fax machine. It's tilted sideways holding his window up.

KEVIN SEAL The concept of *Sporting Fool* in its purest form is taking me and shoving me off something. Whether it was off a bridge, out of an airplane, off a cliff, down the icy luge run. Something about it clicked with America. Whether they wanted to see me die or just be hurt, there was some connection there with the people that I found very rewarding on an emotional level.

JOEL GALLEN Kevin, who is not an athlete at all and doesn't claim to be, would do athletic things. He would jump out of planes. He would jump off bridges. He would compete with very serious athletes and make a fool of himself pretty much, but somehow gracefully, and then introduce videos. It was still another more elaborate way to introduce videos.

We went to Pamplona and ran with the bulls. It's the only episode that had no videos. We had so much good stuff we didn't need the videos. It also won an Ace Award for best recreation and leisure show that year. We were up against *Golf Digest, Fishing with Webber*.

GILBERT GOTTFRIED They would throw him out of planes without a parachute, and have him slam into the sides of buildings. Have him crash cars, set him on fire. And this had nothing to do with anything they were filming. I think that's basically what people wanted to do with Kevin Seal. They wanted to find interesting ways to either torture or kill him.

KEVIN SEAL I think I was the most afraid learning to fly on the trapeze. Just before the trapeze came to me, the guy at the Club Med place confessed that I was his secret fantasy for the week, just before I reached for the bar; just in that instant he said it. Very nice man, extremely charming.

MTV Sports

Dan Cortese

1992–96

DAN CORTESE I was a senior at the University of North Carolina. Janet Jackson was on tour—the Black Cat Tour. I was in a professor's office, arguing about a grade. He got a call from MTV, and they said "We're covering this Janet Jackson concert and we need four or five people to be runners for us. We'll give them fifty dollars and they can see the concert." He hangs up the phone and says, "Do you want to do this?" I do it and meet Robert Laforty.

ROBERT LAFORTY We'd go to a college, to their theater department or their TV department and ask for any good PAs. Dan was a senior about to graduate.

DAN CORTESE After I graduated, I moved to L.A. to be an actor. I needed a job. I called Robert. My first paying gig with MTV was with Ted Demme on *Yo! MTV Raps* down by the L.A. River—which isn't really a river. We were the only white guys there and there was NWA. I had worked with Ted a few other times on *Yo!* Later the West Coast office hired me as an office PA.

PAULY SHORE As a production assistant, he used to hold my stuff on my show. He'd also go get me iced cappuccinos. He watched me, and a year later he's basically doing me—without the pauses. Any time I'm at a party and I see him, he's like, "I did it because of you—you're very inspirational."

DAN CORTESE Then, lo and behold, I was being fired from there after a year and a half due to cutbacks. They happened to have auditions for this new show *MTV Sports*. I got the job and the rest is cable history.

PATRICK BYRNES, producer Our joke was, he was the host of an extreme sports show but he never did anything extreme. He chickened out of skydiving with Matt LeBlanc of *Friends*.

uncensored | 106

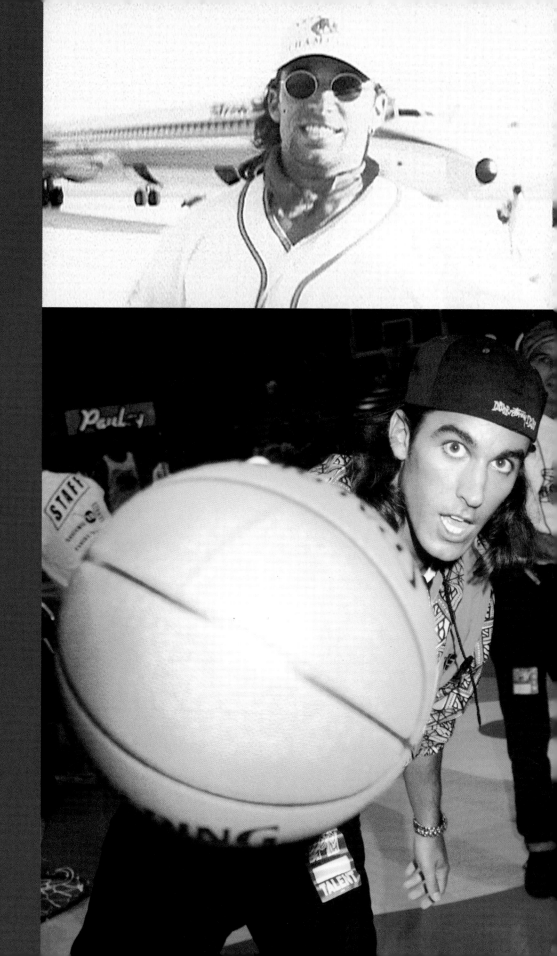

CHRISTINA NORMAN, marketing and promotions executive For the 2000 Video Music Awards campaign, we had to make New York everywhere for the David LaChapelle shoot. Britney was really in San Diego. That's a real New York City cab, though. Jay Z was in Paterson, New Jersey. Lil' Kim was in Brooklyn. *NSYNC was on a stage in Chicago with a giant translight and props and stuff. And Blink-182 was on a New York street on the Universal lot in L.A.

VMA 1988

DATE September 7
LOCATION Universal Amphitheatre, Los Angeles
HOST Arsenio Hall

PERFORMERS

Aerosmith	"Dude Looks Like a Lady"
Cher	"Main Man"
Chubby Checker and the Fat Boys	"Louie, Louie"/ "The Twist"
Crowded House	"Better Be Home Soon"
Depeche Mode	"Strangelove"
Guns N' Roses	"Welcome to the Jungle"
INXS	"New Sensation"
Elton John	"I Don't Wanna Go On With You Like That"
Michael Jackson	"Bad"
Rod Stewart	"Forever Young"
Jody Watley	"Some Kind of Lover"

WINNERS

Best Video	INXS, "Need You Tonight"/"Mediate"
Best Male Video	Prince, "U Got the Look"
Best Female Video	Suzanne Vega, "Luka"
Best Group Video	INXS, "Need You Tonight"
Best New Artist	Guns N' Roses, "Welcome to the Jungle"
Breakthrough Video	INXS, "Need You Tonight"/"Mediate"
Video Vanguard	Michael Jackson
Viewer's Choice	INXS, "Need You Tonight"/"Mediate"

Downtown Julie Brown

1987–92

JULIE BROWN I never got compliments when I was at MTV. I think "bitch" was the nicest thing anyone called me. I think it was like, "Hey there's that nice bitch."

ROB FOX, producer One of the original promo campaigns was "MTV Doodle Doodle Dee wubba wubba wubba." These T-shirts had "Doodle Doodle Dee" on the front and "wubba wubba wubba" on the back. One of the dancers was wearing one of those shirts on the set of *Club MTV*, standing in front of Julie. They were holding up cue cards right above his head. So Julie read down, 'Thanks for being with us here today, I'm Downtown Julie Brown, see ya tomorrow, wubba wubba wubba." We all started cracking up and going, "Julie, you read the kid's T-shirt."

KURT LODER I recall having a couple drinks with Julie Brown one night. Well, probably more than a

couple. She was telling me her story. She had been a kindergarten teacher or something in England. And then she got a job on a kind of traveling disco show that toured Saudi Arabia. How do you do that in a Muslim country? She had a really unusual background.

JULIE BROWN When I got the job, I went to the studio. I went into this dressing room and of course I'm hanging stuff up. There's this beautiful wicker furniture, white wicker. I thought, "Ohhh! This is a nice girl's room." I went in hanging stuff up and Nina comes in. She goes, "Excuse me, but I haven't left yet!" They put me in her room and I felt so bad!

DAISY FUENTES Julie was a crazy wild one, everybody knew it. You couldn't upstage Julie Brown, for goodness' sake. I didn't get a chance to date Billy Idol like she did.

JULIE BROWN Where I came from, it was disco, *Top of the Pops*, Duran Duran. Which was great, but Billy Idol was like, "Whoa, this is fresh. It's so *now*." I was

hanging out with him. I think we kissed a little bit. He's got lovely lips. I'm not gonna tell you everything. But you know what kissing leads to, no matter what your mummy and daddy say. So Billy Idol is probably the only rock 'n' roll person in my house. Unless you heard about some other rumors.

KEVIN SEAL There will never be anyone like her until the Gabor sisters have themselves cloned.

MIKE KILKENNY I used to be Julie Brown's personal assistant back in 1989 for *Club MTV*. Every morning I'd have to buy her personal items before the show. I'd get her a dozen roses, set them up in her room for her. I'd get her Mentos and then I'd wait for her requests throughout the day. Sometimes she might purposely send me out for maxi-pads or tampons or something like that. She is the first girl I ever had to buy those things for and she got me ready for my adulthood. I just wish she remembered my name.

KURT LODER She was born fabulous. Everything was fabulous when she was around.

Club MTV

PREMIERED August 31, 1987

JOE PEROTA, director There was a little delay in the Red Hot Chili Peppers getting to the stage. Flea wanted to come on wearing nothing but a sock over his penis. They wouldn't allow it. There was some discussion as to whether he got on. I can still remember waiting there with the rest of the band. I was standing next to Anthony Kiedis and Chad the drummer. Flea finally came on and he was wearing a pair of long johns. Anthony said, "Wouldn't go for it, huh?" Flea said, "Nah . . ." and they played. We knew they were going to do something special . They proceeded to practically destroy the set. They started climbing up scaffolding, holding up lighting. It was hazardous and dangerous. We were all like, "Oh my God." I was standing underneath. We were talking through our headsets: "They're going to fall. I think we're going to see like major injury here." I still remember the director yelling at the cameras not to miss it. As long as someone's going to get injured, let's make sure we capture it on camera. Thankfully no one got injured. They managed to climb back

down and they had a brief interview with Julie Brown. She got upset and walked off.

ROB FOX My first job was casting director for *Club MTV*. They would send me out to talk to pretty women at bars. I was the envy of all my friends. Howard Stern would call me in the morning. He thought I had the greatest job in the world. The most interesting part of being the casting director for *Club MTV*. I was also a panty monitor. We had a set of rules that any woman or girl dancing on the platforms had to wear panties, because of the infamous up-skirt shots of *Club MTV*. Someone, I'm sure, somewhere, has a director's reel of boobs falling out of low-cut dresses and shots. I would get on the headsets: "Rob, uh, we really need you to take that girl off the platform because I can see her hairstyle and I'm not talking about her head."

On the *Club MTV* Tour, one of the classic, classic pieces of footage, is Milli Vanilli coming out to "Girl You Know It's True." And they come out, and literally the CD of their vocals is skipping. They're onstage in front of ten thousand people and the vocals are

skipping. They run back, and they come back out, and it starts skipping again. Finally they just lose it and take off and that was kind of the beginning of the end for Milli Vanilli's reign in the sun.

JULIE BROWN They were putting out music you could dance to, so MTV wasn't saying, "This is dance music," they were saying, "This is music you can dance to—have fun with it." It was basically club stuff. You know, when you go out, it wasn't just one particular song or one particular flavor that was out there. And so I became the little dance diva, and *Club MTV* was born. And there we were, picking chicks with big knockers and gorgeous looks and, you know, if they'd come in with a skirt down there, I'd hike it up a little bit, because then to be sexy wasn't wearing a bikini or wearing a pair of shorts and having your boobs hanging out. Being sexy was just being a girl and having fun, or being a guy and having fun, taking your shirt off and just dancing.

VMA 1990

DATE September 6
LOCATION Universal Amphitheatre, Los Angeles
HOST Arsenio Hall

PERFORMERS

2 Live Crew	"Banned in the USA"
Aerosmith	"Love in an Elevator"
Phil Collins	"Sussudio"
Faith No More	"Epic"
INXS	"Suicide Blonde"
Janet Jackson	"Black Cat"
Madonna	"Vogue"
M. C. Hammer	"U Can't Touch This"
Mötley Crüe	"Don't Go Away Mad"
New Edition featuring Bobby Brown	"Poison"/"Tap Into My Heart"/ "Rub You the Right Way"/ "Sensitivity"/"If It Isn't Love"/"Mr. Telephone Man"/ "Can You Stand the Rain"
Sinéad O'Connor	"Nothing Compares 2 U"
World Party	"Put the Message in the Box"

WINNERS

Best Video	Sinéad O'Connor, "Nothing Compares 2 U"
Best Male Video	Don Henley, "End of the Innocence"
Best Female Video	Sinéad O'Connor, "Nothing Compares 2 U"
Best Group Video	The B-52's, "Love Shack"
Best Rap Video	M. C. Hammer, "U Can't Touch This"
Best Dance Video	M. C. Hammer, "U Can't Touch This"
Best Metal/ Hard Rock Video	Aerosmith, "Janie's Got a Gun"
Best New Artist	Michael Penn, "No Myth"
Breakthrough Video	Tears for Fears, "Sowing the Seeds of Love"
Viewer's Choice	Aerosmith, "Janie's Got a Gun"
Video Vanguard	Janet Jackson

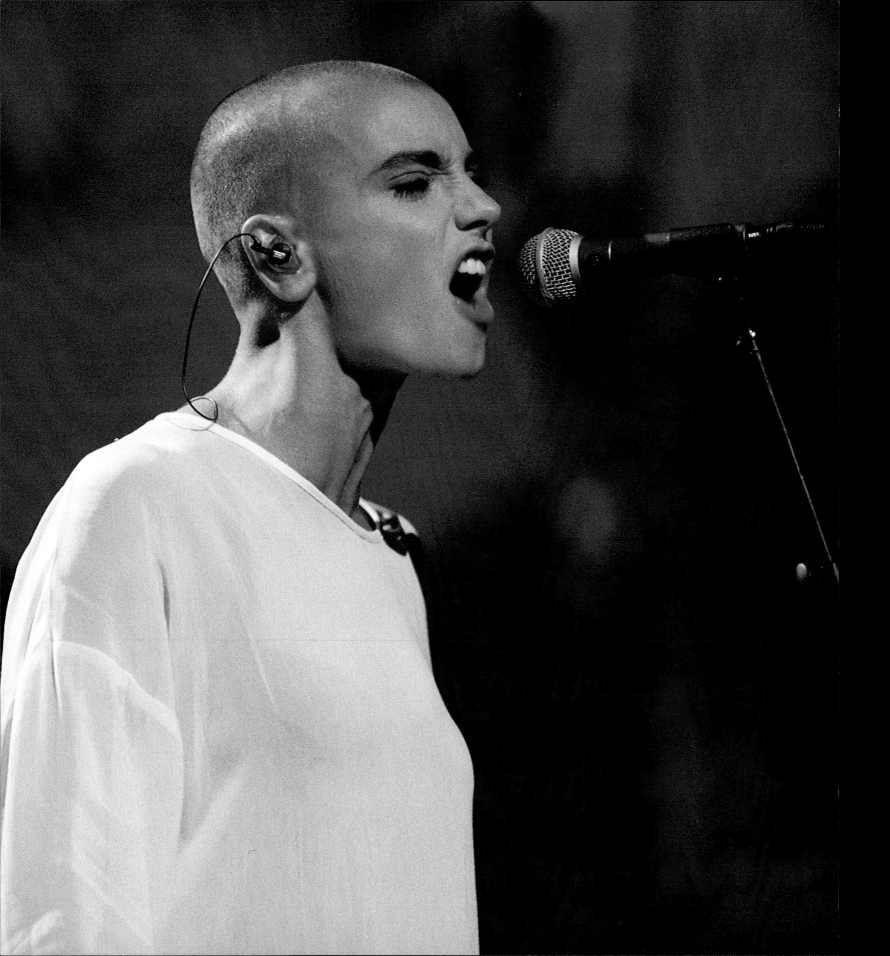

SUICIDAL TENDENCIES & ANTHRAX

Headbanger's Ball

LARS ULRICH If we were too hung over from a Friday night and stayed home Saturday night, it was always interesting to see what they would dig up for the *Headbanger's Ball*.

SEBASTIAN BACH Midnight on Saturdays, we'd get together, get a case of beer, and watch *Headbanger's Ball*. It was the greatest.

TOM MORELLO The show that was the be-all and end-all was *Headbanger's Ball*. When I moved to California we'd go to Sunset BBQ and on Saturday night they would play *Headbanger's Ball* on the little TV screens and we'd watch and study the latest gestures and gyrations of Poison and Skid Row.

SLASH I think the first experience on *Headbanger's Ball* was when we destroyed the stage. They told us that we would, and they were kind of kidding, and we tore the set up.

Rikki Rachtman

1990–95

RIKKI RACHTMAN I had received a bit of notoriety in Los Angeles because of some nightclubs that I opened. One was called the Cat House and it became notorious because of the bands that started there and the celebrities that hung out at the club. Everybody from Michelle Pfeiffer to George Michael to every rock star and porno star you could imagine. I was friends with the guys in Guns N' Roses at that time, and one night I was watching *Headbanger's Ball* with Axl and I was like, "Dude, I wanna do that." And he was like, "Want me to call somebody? You'd be good." And I'd hate to say it's one of those who-you-know things, but hey, I'll take it when I can get it. Axl called some people at MTV and set up an audition and he said, "If you go to New York, I'll go to New York with you." So I went to my audition with Axl Rose and I guess it didn't hurt.

MARILYN MANSON I think Twiggy and I were making out in front of Rikki Rachtman. He seemed very intimidated by our ambiguous sexual appearance.

VMA 1989

DATE September 6
LOCATION Universal Amphitheatre, Los Angeles
HOST Arsenio Hall

PERFORMERS

Paula Abdul	"Straight Up"/"Forever Your Girl"/"Cold-Hearted Snake" (medley)
Bobby Brown	"On Our Own"
Jon Bon Jovi and Richie Sambora	"Wanted Dead or Alive"/ "Livin' on a Prayer"
Cher	"If I Could Turn Back Time"
The Cult	"Live"
Def Leppard	"Tear It Down"
Madonna	"Express Yourself"
Tom Petty and the Heartbreakers with Axl Rose	"Free Fallin'"/"Heartbreak Hotel"
The Cure	"Just Like Heaven"
The Rolling Stones	"Mixed Emotions"
Tone-Lōc	"Wild Thing"

WINNERS

Best Video	Neil Young, "This Note's for You"
Best Male Video	Elvis Costello, "Veronica"
Best Female Video	Paula Abdul, "Straight Up"
Best Group Video	Living Colour, "Cult of Personality"
Best Rap Video	DJ Jazzy Jeff and the Fresh Prince, "Parents Just Don't Understand"
Best Heavy Metal Video	Guns N' Roses, "Sweet Child of Mine"
Best New Artist	Living Colour, "Cult of Personality"
Video Vanguard	George Michael
Viewer's Choice	Madonna, "Like a Prayer"

JOE DAVOLA, former executive David Lee Roth was up for a ton of awards. Him and Van Halen. And they won none. So I went backstage and stole one of the awards. And sent it to his house for him, because I felt bad. They had a ton of them backstage with none of the names on them. So I just put one in my bag, went over to his room at the Parker Meridien hotel and said, "Here, this is from everybody at MTV, you deserve one, even though you're getting it as a gift."

JOEL GALLEN, producer MTV told me to strive for one surprise every half hour, which is sort of impossible—it's like five or six surprises. The opening of the show was Madonna singing "Express Yourself." There was no introduction, no laundry list of who is going to be on the show. We just faded up from black, the curtain opened, and there was Madonna behind a screen in silhouette. Cold open. The place just went nuts and it set the tone for a show with surprises.

SEBASTIAN BACH I was sitting right in front of them and they looked at me right before they did it. They did a great job. I think Bon Jovi started the whole unplugged thing with that performance.

Spring Break

CARSON DALY Before I worked here, I hated it. I couldn't afford to go to these places. I was never gonna go to Jamaica, never gonna go to Cancún. I had my spring break, which was like four or five days, or ten days, however hell long it was. And I just sat there watching MTV and just resented them and everybody down there. And I just thought, "I hate you."

PATRICK BYRNES My first "paid" MTV gig was PA-ing the very first MTV *Spring Break* in '86. Somehow I got assigned to making sure Les Garland [VP of talent] got around town safely. Funny thing was, we first met in a bar. I came to hang with him and Dana Marshall and John Cannelli and then drive them home because Les partied *hard*.

Well, we're hanging out for an hour and he's forcing drinks on me and being very cool. I'm the new guy hangin' with the head of the company and thinking, "Boy, is this wild." At some point, John Cannelli leans in on me, laughing, and says, "He thinks you're one of the Beastie Boys. Dude, play along."

KEN OBER Gilbert Gottfried was there every year. The one thing I'll always remember about Gilbert is the way he dressed to go. We were in Daytona Beach and when it wasn't raining, it would be eighty or ninety degrees and Gilbert would have black dress pants on, black shoes, dark socks, different colors on each foot, a dark shirt as though he was going to give a deposition at a law office, and he'd be on the beach dressed like that every year. And nobody ever wanted to go over to him and say, "Gilbert, do you want to borrow a pair of shorts or something?"

GILBERT GOTTFRIED There was one *Spring Break* where they had a model there and she was a top model at that time period who shall remain nameless, but no it's not the one with the mole and that's all I'm telling you. But it was a top model and I remember about like a year later everybody was telling me, "Hey, remember that model? Boy, she slept with everybody. She slept with everybody on MTV and then when she was through with the guys on MTV she was with every guy on the beach." And I don't know, I mean I guess when she hit my room she was probably tired by then. I can only fantasize that she was right about to knock on my door when she just collapsed from exhaustion.

CARSON DALY Most things I've experienced here at MTV have been scaled down from what I thought they would be. For instance, if I saw a Green Day concert on MTV, or the Video Music Awards, I would have thought, "Wow that's the coolest thing." And then when you actually go and see what it's all about, it's always a little bit watered down. You know, it's not all it's cracked up to be. It's not what you see on TV.

Spring Break is the only thing that's the other way around. Half the stuff that happens at *Spring Break* never airs.

DAN CORTESE *Spring Break* is just *nuts*. It looks nuts on air, but it's a hundred times more nuts off air. We went to Daytona Beach for five days to work on it and they had us under aliases at the hotel. At the time I was there with my girlfriend, who is now my wife. And we'd come back from outside working and she'd be taking messages off the phone, "Michelle from the fifth floor called and said that you can come down anytime."

JANEANE GAROFALO I went to *Spring Break* a couple of times. It's great, but at the time even when I started it was much more fly-by-the-seat-of-your-pants youth-staffed MTV. I mean now it's like a well-oiled machine. I can remember, and I don't know if anyone will admit to this, but they used to have garbage cans of planter's punch around on the beach that the crew was helping themselves to and stuff like that. I think they don't do that anymore. I think the alcohol policy has been enforced with MTV now.

JIMMY HANRAHAN, wardrobe You're in a sea of thousands of drunk kids at a topless bar. It's like when we were in Jamaica, there were girls that, literally, for like a twenty-five-dollar prize, were stripping naked in these wet T-shirt contests. Tops, bottoms, humping on the nearest drunk guy. I'm going, "This is twenty-five dollars, honey. It's two in the afternoon."

CAMILLE GRAMMER, dancer Everybody was hitting on everyone. I mean, the executives were hitting on the dancers. It was just crazy. It was everybody flirting with everyone else. Even the rock stars, musicians that came down, they were hitting on some of the dancers.

I remember one of the guys from Ugly Kid Joe projectile-vomiting off the balcony of the Marriott hotel. I remember the same person, I'm not going to say which band member it was, saying he had to jump offstage during rehearsal to throw up in a planter on the side of the stage. Because everybody just drank hard. Everybody just partied hard. So you know, by the time everybody was ready to perform or rehearse, everybody was either hung over or completely annihilated. So, yeah, it was fun.

FOXY BROWN I had a white Gucci bikini and I popped out everywhere. And I was like, "Ahh," and they were just cheering along, and I was rapping like this [hand covering breast]. So that was fun. That was the first time I had been to anything like that so it was such a great experience for me. Basically the *Spring Break* crowd is the best 'cause they just pump you up.

CARSON DALY I've seen everything. Last year, in Jamaica, we walked down to the beach. Me and Rebecca Romijn-Stamos and John Stamos, her husband, walked around and checked out the hot tubs and there was just like full-blown orgies. Lots of old people naked, just kind of disgusting. But no one cares. Just total *Spring Break* vibe. A lot of drinking. We went to a bar in Negril and it's just packed,

packed, packed. Jay-Z was there hanging out. A lot of celebrities just kind of doing their thing. And people, kids, just clawing at them. And once the music's on, it's just the most intense party I've ever seen.

I went to the hotel and I heard a little commotion in the bar and I heard a couple of people singing and whatnot, figured it was coworkers, went up to my room, got my bags, went to the hotel bar. And it was a bunch of people I work with and at the piano were Jordan Knight and Joey MacIntyre, who had had a few. And they were singing some old soul songs around the piano. And it's one of those moments where you realize the dream of every fourteen-year-old of the world is being lived by a twenty-seven-year-old guy. So yeah, I hung out. I did not sing along with them. A lot of people think that we go down, or maybe I go down, and, you know, I go to bars and go crazy and hook up with girls and, you know, it's really not like that. The shooting schedule, especially for me, I ended up doing everything. I was like, "Where's Dave, where's Ananda? Can't they do something?" I need to start drinking beer and living it up in Mexico, this is my one shot to be in Cancún that I don't have to pay for.

It was just pouring down rain and I remember hearing Bush fight with the MTV people. "We're not going to go out there and fucking play in this rain." And the MTV people were like, "Look, if anything happens to your equipment we'll pay for it." I just remember them arguing and thinking, "This is cool, this is rock 'n' roll." And then they were on a big weather hold because of lightning, and I can remember Bush getting out there. I didn't actually see Gavin fall or hit his tooth on the mic or whatever, but apparently he did and lost his tooth, and they flew him to L.A. that night to have cosmetic surgery. He had to rejoin the No Doubt tour, I think is what it was at the time.

TOMMY CODY, writer At *Spring Break* 2000 in Cancún, I was backstage when our wardrobe/makeup guy came out of a dressing room. He looked a little stunned, and extremely anxious to tell us something. *"Oh my God, you guys!"*

He told us that he walked in on a lead singer having sex with a socialite. As he told us the story, the socialite was on all fours at the moment they were discovered, but she just lifted one hand off the floor and said, "Busy!"

They were still at it when he walked out.

CARSON DALY *Spring Break Fashionably Loud* was the first time I ever met Limp Bizkit. I think it really put them on the map. What was their deal? They flew in for like a day or something and they were all stoked because they were on a jet or something like that. They were really cool. They were really happy to be there and just completely partaking.

There's a guy who'll party his ass off, Fred Durst. I guarantee you that if I had to pick one rock icon, one guy who you'll see on an *MTV Spring Break* with chicks, with alcohol, having the best time, it will be Fred from Limp Bizkit. And I hope I'm not too far behind him.

VMA 2000

DATE September 7
LOCATION Radio City Music Hall, New York
HOST Shawn and Marlon Wayans

PERFORMERS

*NSYNC	"This I Promise You"/"Bye, Bye, Bye"/"It's Gonna Be Me"
Britney Spears	"Satisfaction"/"Oops . . . I Did It Again"
Janet Jackson	"Doesn't Really Matter"
Rage Against the Machine	"Testify"
Eminem	"The Real Slim Shady"/"The Way I Am"
Blink-182	"All the Small Things"
Red Hot Chili Peppers	"Californication"
Nelly	"Country Grammar"
Sisqo	"Incomplete"/"Thong Song"
Christina Aguilera	"Genie in a Bottle"/"Come On Over Baby"

WINNERS

Best Video	Eminem, "The Real Slim Shady"
Best Male Video	Eminem, "The Real Slim Shady"
Best Female Video	Aaliyah, "Try Again"
Best Group Video	Blink-182, "All the Small Things"
Best Rap Video	Dr. Dre with Eminem, "Forgot About Dre"
Best Dance Video	Jennifer Lopez, "Waiting for Tonight"
Best Hip-Hop Video	Sisqo, "Thong Song"
Best Rock Video	Limp Bizkit, "Break Stuff"
Best Pop Video	*NSYNC, "Bye, Bye, Bye"
Best New Artist in a Video	Macy Gray, "I Try"
Best Video from a Film	Aaliyah, "Try Again"
Best R&B Video	Destiny's Child, "Say My Name"
Viewer's Choice Award	*NSYNC, "Bye, Bye, Bye"
Breakthrough Video	Björk, "All Is Full of Love"

CHRIS CONNELLY Someone had told me that Britney's number was really gonna knock a few socks off. Then we were rehearsing our pre-show the same time Britney was rehearsing her number, so I was in the Radio City balcony when she came down the stairs. When she got her outfit ripped off and she started dancing, I think everyone in the place did a silent "wow." I still tell people the rehearsal was even better than the actual performance.

BRIAN GRADEN, president, production and programming We're living in the pop era and we're working with a lot of very nice stars. But they are also competitive people. So the demeanor backstage was really pretty friendly and everybody gives big hugs. We had done a *TRL* photo shoot a few months before and Christina and Britney were talking like old friends—but you can tell. When they call you and tell you what they want to do with their performance, they want to make it just absolutely spectacular because they want to do the best job at least on equal par with all the other artists. So the competition is there. It's just not as blatant as it used to be.

CHRIS CONNELLY We were on the Radio City marquee getting ready for the post-show when the Tim C. [of Rage Against the Machine] thing went down. I think Brian was the only guy on the team who was still in the house when it happened, so we spent a lot of the minutes leading up to the post-show just grilling him for details. We probably saw less of it than anyone, and there we were, having to talk about it right away!

LUKE PELLEGRINI It was about two in the morning. We were there all night, practicing, rehearsing, for Eminem. Locked up like chickens in a coop on the stairs of Radio City Music Hall. And after we were finally done rehearsing I got the chance to go and talk to Eminem for a couple of minutes. And we're in Radio City Music Hall and a couple other of the wanna-be Slim Shadys came up to also talk to Eminem. Not too many. We're in Radio City. We're not regular people. We're helping him out. And in

midsentence people came to shake his hand and he was just like, "Guys, I don't have hands for everybody." He got behind his bodyguard and walked away, like a little bitch. He totally copped out. This was disturbing 'cause we were helping him out basically for free. We liked him. He just was a punk about it, and really didn't talk to anyone. Dre came out and spent half an hour with everybody, talked to everybody, took pictures, and was totally cool. I lost respect for Eminem after.

Beach House

DAVE HOLMES MTV Beach House is like summer vacation that everybody gets to go on. It's filmed in a way that you really feel like you're there. You're at your friends' house. My first gig was at the Beach House in Seaside Heights. I just thought I'd get a room and Ananda would be down the hall and sometimes she'd have to buy the toothpaste and sometimes I would. It's really not like that.

ADAM FREEMAN, producer In 1993, MTV was sponsoring a contest to win Dr. Dre's low-rider featured in many of his videos. The car was delivered to the Hamptons via truck and I had to pick it up and drive it back to the Beach House. When I arrived in East Hampton I realized that Dr. Dre obviously had the car repainted after shooting the videos because it now featured airbrushed murals of naked ho's and a clown smoking crack. I had to drive this car through the ritzy Hamptons during a street fair when traffic was five m.p.h. and every family was on the street. Halfway through the fair it started to rain. Fumbling for the switch to put the convertible top up, I accidentally triggered the hydraulics and was now *bouncing* a crack clown/ho-painted car through the streets of South Hampton while upper-class snotty Hampton people covered their kids' faces and cursed at me.

CARSON DALY Kennedy used to bust my balls all the time. There was one time we were doing a segment at Motel California and she was just killing me. Like, "Oh, you're daddy's little boy who owns the country club," or something like that. And I kept coming back with stuff and after we'd cut she was like, "You're not allowed to do that! You're the new guy."

KENNEDY Carson really should have been through more of a boot camp. He really needed to learn how to toughen up. We'd hide his clothes, we made him eat dumb stuff, and we made fun of him. We called him candy. Candy Daly. Candy Susie. It was all out of love. I think he handled it like a champ. I think his true colors really showed through that summer.

ADAM FREEMAN Radiohead performed live at the Beach House to promote their first album. We built them a stage over the inground pool. At the end of one song singer Thom Yorke got very excited and dove into the pool. Unfortunately he forgot he had combat boots on and immediately sank to the bottom. Two coworkers and I were the only ones to notice he wasn't coming back up.

JEN PALCHINSKY, producer He said something like, "My boots turned into cement shoes."

ADAM FREEMAN He finally popped up near the stage frantically trying to grab something to pull himself up with. We reached out our hands as he decided the live mic wire was a better option. He grabbed it and was just about to be shocked to death before we slapped it out of his hand and grabbed him by the shirt and pulled him out. I think we are solely responsible for the rest of their career.

20 Questions for 20 Years

TOM DELONGE OF BLINK-182

What song best describes your current state of mind?
"I'm Too Sexy for My…"

What is favorite video of all time?
Beastie Boys, "Sabotage"

What is your first memory of MTV?
The horrible moon man animation over and over again.

Where were you the first time you saw yourself on MTV and how did you react?
In my girlfriend's house, we laughed and I think I got some that night.

Does the video enhance or hinder the song?
It enhances by helping the band visualize what their point of view is.

What is the most memorable moment you've witnessed on MTV?
Us winning the VMA 2000—I was there, I saw it with my own two eyes

Whose video work do you most admire?
Spike Jonze

What do you like most about MTV?
Every once and a while they play videos

What do you like least about MTV?
They only play videos every once and a while

What is your favorite guilty pleasure video?
Anything with half- naked ladies

What do you consider to be MTV's greatest achievement and/or greatest failure in its first 20 years?
Becoming a musical giant that can propel bands to great status. And having nudity and bad words.

What is the worst reaction you've received to one of your videos?
Lots of horny men thinking we are a little gay

Videos should…
Be entertaining and tell the story of the song in the artists eyes.

The best band name
Blink-182

The greatest moment in Rock and Pop and Rap was
This question takes way too much thinking. I would rather take this time to promote my future solo album, "Sexy Asshole"

My biggest influence
"The Descendents"

My favorite VMA performance
Backstreet boys coming down on rocket surfboards

If I were President of MTV I would…
Run shows on UFOs and test television standards with soft-core porn.

What artist would you most like to work with and what would you like to do with them?
I want to do a punk rock ensemble with the Beastie Boys—or shoot an erotic video with Madonna.

Did video kill the radio star?
Look at Dan Cortex—video had sex with the radio star.

Jon Stewart

1993–95

JON STEWART *You Wrote It, You Watch It* was the first thing we did at MTV. It seemed like a good idea at the time. We got letters from viewers and then our sketch troupe acted them out. The shows got bizarre. Ninety percent of the letters were somebody throwing up on an animal. People didn't—what's the word I'm looking for—"watch it." Basically the show could be called *You Wrote It*. Because the second part was really the key, that you watch it. People never got that.

After that show ended, I was sent to Sicily to chill out for a while, like the Godfather. Some of us were having dinner one night. Someone had brought beer and we were all a little hammered. They asked if I have any ideas for some shows for the network. I said, "Well how about this show? Let's try and find out what happens when people stop being polite and start getting nervous." They didn't go for that. Then I think I said, "How about a talk show?" And they said, "Okay."

The first guest on the talk show was Howard Stern. I had stayed up all night the night before. I was very nervous. I had never met him before, but I was very excited 'cause I was a big fan. I thought of every angle he was going to go on. I can handle this. I'm a smart guy, a funny guy. He came on the show, walks out and he goes, "I don't know who you are and you're going to be off the air in six weeks." God, I was like that guy in the Maxell commercial. Faced.

Howard was just nailing me left and right. I did the only thing I could do. I just flipped open his book and I go, "What's this chapter on lesbians?" Woo. He was off me. That's what I still do with every guest. Sometimes it works, sometimes it doesn't.

Anna Nicole Smith was a very interesting case. I was used to viewers falling asleep during the show. This was the first time we had a guest do it. You'd ask a question and then you'd begin to see the reflex of trying to answer. She was definitely trying to hang in there. About halfway through it she'd go, "What was the question?" When we went to commercial—I had never seen this before—she had like an Indy pit crew with her. All of a sudden eight guys come out, hydraulics, put her on a jack, twisting her head around, slapping her around, and there's just one lady in the front going, "Come on, you can do this." We came back and she was a little fresher.

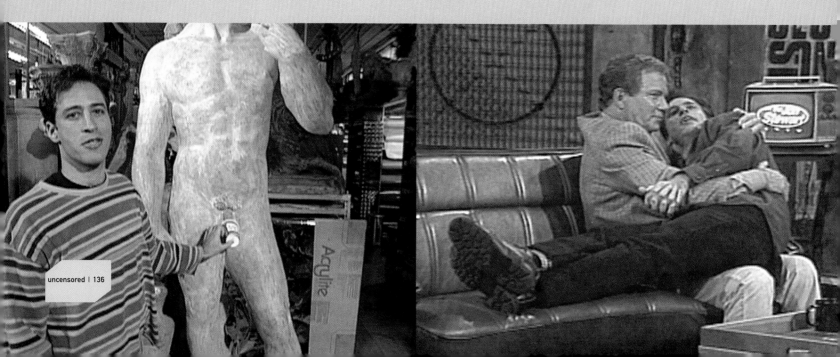

RZA That's where MTV News comes in handy. The artists don't feel shy to speak on it, they know it's their community. You get more freedom from the artist. They interviewed Wu Tang many times and we sat there, we talked openly. We know that's going right to our people.

ICE-T I think MTV News is like one of the best shows, you know? 'Cause it gives you a quick blurb. And I think people in the music business want to know what's going on inside the music business.

Week in Rock

LINDA CORRADINA The original "Week in Rock" was a package that we used to run every week. It was, "On Monday, Mötley Crüe made a video. On Tuesday, Van Halen got into a fight. On Wednesday, There was a riot at a concert in Milwaukee." It was every day and it ran in rotation.

DOUG HERZOG, former executive Once we started doing *MTV News* and generating a lot of news on a weekly and daily basis, we had writers, we had producers, we thought, "Well, why don't we just put it all together and wrap it up in a weekly half-hour?" It seemed like kind of a logical no-brainer. That's really what it was: to take everything we did and put it together, see if we could get people to watch it for a half-hour. Before we did that, news wasn't really done for ratings, it was sort of done for credibility.

DAVE SIRULNICK, executive producer We knew that the news department as well as the show needed an identity and all the VJs rotated in and out: Julie Brown hosted "Week in Rock," Kevin Seal, Adam Curry did it for a long time, and it was okay, but you just knew that for the show to take off you needed one person.

KEVIN SEAL For a while, I hosted "Week in Rock," but the last time I did it, it was discovered that I had been without my pants on. And from that point forward, Kurt took over. You'd have to ask him about that. Kurt kept his pants on.

KURT LODER We didn't know what the show was. I was totally at sea. I mean, I had no idea. I don't think I looked my best then. I'm sure we worked on me after that.

DAVE SIRULNICK When "Week in Rock" first went on, everybody that works on a show like that, you sort of wonder if anybody's watching. You wonder if anybody out there is watching besides your friends or your parents or something. Slowly but surely you would start to hear, when you do an interview with a band or you're out covering a concert, you'd start to hear, "I saw that on 'Week in Rock,'" and you'd go back to the newsroom and tell everyone, "Yeah! Somebody saw what we did!" Things changed when we hired Kurt Loder and he became our anchor.

All of a sudden it had respectability.

20 Questions for 20 Years

AL YANKOVIC

What song best describes your current state of mind?
"Dare to Be Stupid."

What is favorite video of all time?
The video that my parents made all of our old 8mm home movies.

What is your first memory of MTV?
I didn't have cable TV for a long time, so I just kept hearing rumors about this mysterious channel that would play Night Ranger videos every hour.

Where were you the first time you saw yourself on MTV and how did you react?
I was in front of a TV set, and I think I said something like, "Hey! I'm on TV!"

Does the video enhance or hinder the song?
It usually enhances it. I mean, think of all the subtleties in the "Thong Song" that you'd just miss if you didn't see the accompanying video.

What is the most memorable moment you've witnessed on MTV?
For some reason, I can't get the image of Tom Green humping a dead moose out of my head.

Whose video work do you most admire?
Mark Romanek, Spike Jonze, Stephen Johnson.

What do you like most about MTV?
They helped me buy my house.

What do you like least about MTV?
I wish they hadn't given J.J. Jackson my home phone number.

What is your favorite guilty pleasure video?
Teletubbies—especially their early stuff.

What do you consider to be MTV's greatest achievement and/or greatest failure in its first 20 years?
For better or worse, MTV has made it nearly impossible to think of a hit song without also thinking about its accompanying video images.

What is the worst reaction you've received to one of your videos?
I hear Coolio wasn't too pleased with "Amish Paradise."

Videos should . . .
Feature as many midgets as the budget will allow.

The best band name is
Jesus Chrysler.

The greatest moment in rock and pop and rap was . . .
The invention of electricity.

My biggest influence is
John Tesh.

My favorite VMA performance
Pee Wee Herman introducing the show that one year.

If I were president of MTV I would . . .
Insist that Weird Al videos be played 24/7.

What artist would you most like to work with and what would you like to do with them?
Madonna—I'd like her to help me paint my house.

Did video kill the radio star?
No, but it gave him a really bad wedgie.

Kurt Loder

1988–present

RZA Kurt, I mean, everybody loves Kurt. Kurt Loder. Hey, he's a friend of mine, too. You know what I mean?

LINDA CORRADINA We used to get so frustrated in news. We would work all day on the scripts, deliver them and the VJs would just mess up the copy. And we were like, "Can't we have our own newsreader?"

JOE PEROTA, director We'd see the copy and say, "Julie will never be able to say that. Change that word."

DAVE SIRULNICK We wanted to take the news department to a new level. We wanted to be able to report on the news, to be able to break stories. We knew to do that we had to have somebody who the audience could identify with and trust.

KURT LODER I was sitting in my office at *Rolling Stone* one day and Linda Corradina, who was the head of the news department at the time, just called me up and asked me if I'd like a job. I had been working there for nine years at *RS*.

LINDA CORRADINA I was half-shocked that he was even listening. I'm thinking, "This guy is never going to leave.' But I really liked his writing, and I thought, "Let's just see."

He was like, "What should I wear?" His clothes were these loud polyester shirts. Brown and green and paisley.

I actually remember sitting in the back of the control room, wanting to like him, because I knew how good he was. I just remember going, "He's not terrible."

DAVE SIRULNICK We were really settled on someone who had experience. We were saying to everybody, "Tell us about the first concert you ever went to."

Everybody would go on about the first concert they ever went to. Kurt just sort of looked at us, and he says, "I can't remember the first concert I ever went to, what, are you kidding me?" He's like, "I've been to a million concerts, I can't remember." He just was like, "Take me as I am—this is it. You know what I do, you've read my stuff." Just take it or leave it.

KURT LODER I did this camera test. Probably a disaster, I would imagine. And they hired me. That was it—very simple.

ALEX COLETT, producer I floor-produced his audition. Based on his audition, I might not have hired him, had it been my decision. Linda was a lot smarter than I was. Kurt wore a striped shirt. They put a lot of makeup on him and he sweated. He was

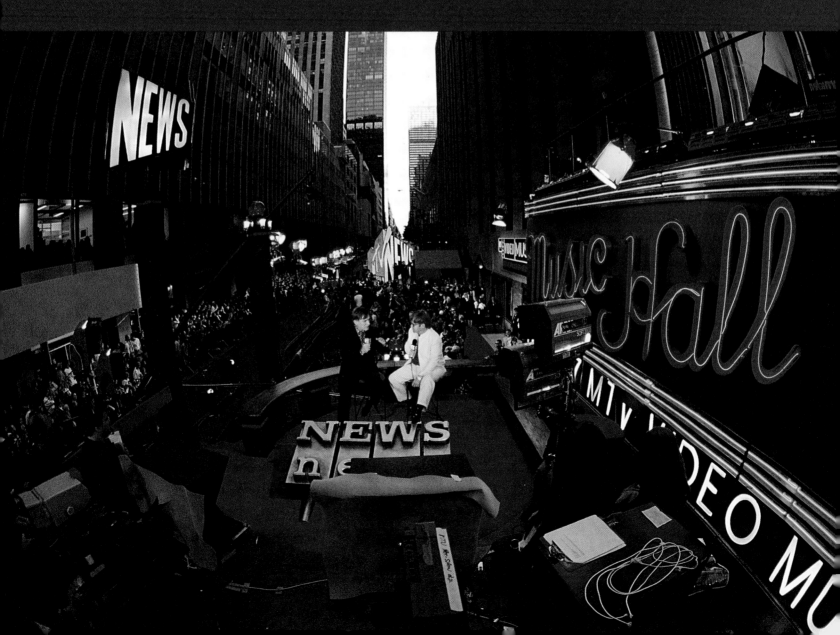

sweating profusely. Makeup runs, so by the end of it he looked like Iggy Pop after a show.

CHRIS CONNELLY They signed Kurt and that was a big deal, you know. Kurt had actual credibility so that meant they were going to do something interesting, because no one could get Kurt to say anything he didn't want to say.

ADAM CURRY VJs did the news when we first started off. My credibility was shot to hell the minute Kurt came in. Kurt had a lot of personal relationships through his *Rolling Stone* background. From then on, news just took control of all of the cool stuff. All of the good interviews went to *MTV News*.

KURT LODER The first time I went on it was some sort of gathering of famous people somewhere. There was a wardrobe lady who said "Well, you have to wear something MTV-ish." She gave me this really tatty, fab, electric-blue jacket, with this band across the back and great big shoulder pads. This was so embarrassing. I just felt so bad. I wore it to this thing and was just hanging my head, I felt so terrible. After

that I didn't deal with wardrobe anymore at all. I wasn't going to let them do that to me.

DAVE SIRULNICK One of the first times we ever went out shooting, we're covering Bruce Springsteen launching a tour in the winter of '88. It's freezing cold. I have him outside interviewing fans. Kurt had never done anything like this on camera before. We get the footage of Bruce and we go to the edit afterward. I say to Kurt, "OK, I'm going to look at the footage. You sit down and start writing the script."

A few minutes later he hands me a script, first script he's ever written for MTV. "Bruce Springsteen took the stage resplendent in a white shirt, black jeans, black boots and a silver buckle." He goes on for about four sentences describing what Bruce Springsteen looked like. I said, "Kurt, this is television, we can see what he looks like, let's get right to what he did." You saw this lightbulb go on over his head and he says, "Right, got it!" After that, he just became a master at playing off of the nuances that he saw on camera and of the footage that we had.

JOHN NORRIS Well, this is a weird thing. If there is anyone out there who can give me any idea as to why this happens, I'm dying to know, but for years now I get recognized all the time. But I'd say eight out of ten people who know my face say, "Kurt, what's up? Kurt Loder, how you doin'? Kurt, Mr. MTV." At this point, I've stopped correcting them.

CINDY CRAWFORD Kurt is just Kurt. And he's got that dry, really smart sense of humor. And sometimes you're not sure if he's making fun of you, or you're supposed to laugh with him, or he's laughing at you. You're not really sure. I was very intimated by Kurt in the beginning. But of course, like a typical twenty-two-year-old, instead of going, "Nice to meet you, Mr. Loder," I think I was a smart-ass to him, dissing his fashion sense or something. I walked into his office, and I'm sure it's because I was really nervous and intimidated, but I think I was giving him a hard time. Over the years we got to know each other and work together. Hopefully there's a mutual respect, 'cause I definitely respect him. He's so much a part of MTV.

All the real work in television is done by producers, and no producer I've ever met has worked harder than Dave Sirulnick, a man who's willing to do anything short of Murder One to get the shot he wants. One sweltering day in L.A., Dave decided it would be really cool to shoot a standup at the famous Hollywood sign—by which he meant: standing right next to it. Unfortunately, there was no way to simply drive up to the thing at the top of the mountain (well, okay, "hill") on which it was situated. So Dave determined that we would climb up instead. This was no problem for our cameraman that day, who turned out to be a mountaineer in his spare time—he bounded up through the brush and the dirt and the crumbling rock at a breathtaking pace, while Dave and I, in classic New Yorker style, panted along behind, inhaling his dust and collapsing every few yards to clutch at our wildly pounding hearts. After an hour and a half, we reached the top, where we were greeted not just by the cameraman, who seemed barely to have broken a sweat, but by an agent of the FBI, who informed us that the mini-Everest atop which we were finally standing actually housed a high-security federal communications base, and that we were trespassing.

Thinking with remarkable alacrity for a man on the verge of myocardial infarction, Dave explained to the FBI guy that we were shooting *Week in Rock*—surely he knew of it?—and if the agent would just pretend he hadn't seen us, and wander away for a bit while we shot our little segment, he could have the clutch of free MTV promotional T-shirts we always carried with us for bribing purposes. The agent agreed, we got our shot, and we lived to forswear any further such exertion in the future.

—KURT LODER

JOEL GALLEN The best rock 'n' roll performance in the history of the Video Music Awards. Pearl Jam performed onstage, and then—this was a surprise—after they did their song, "Animal," they brought out Neil Young, completely unannounced. We didn't even know for sure if he was gonna show up. He didn't come to rehearsal. About fifteen minutes before they were scheduled to go on, we got word that he was backstage. He just plugged in and did this incredible version of "Rockin' in the Free World." The place went crazy. It was just one of those moments, one of those live music moments that I think people talk about.

VMA 1993

Tenth Anniversary Show

DATE September 2
LOCATION Universal Amphitheatre, Los Angeles
HOST Christian Slater

PERFORMERS

Aerosmith	"Livin' on the Edge"
The Edge from U2	"Numb"
Janet Jackson	"That's the Way Love Goes"/"If"
Lenny Kravitz	"Are You Gonna Go My Way?"
Madonna	"Bye Bye Baby"
Naughty by Nature	"Hip Hop Hooray"
Pearl Jam	"Animal"
Pearl Jam and Neil Young	"Rockin' in the Free World"
R.E.M.	"Everybody Hurts"/"Drive"
Soul Asylum w/ Peter Buck and Victoria Williams	"Runaway Train"
Spin Doctors	"Two Princes"
Sting	"If I Ever Lose My Faith in You"

WINNERS

Best Video	Pearl Jam, "Jeremy"
Best Male Video	Lenny Kravitz, "Are You Gonna Go My Way?"
Best Female Video	k.d. lang, "Constant Craving"
Best Group Video	Pearl Jam, "Jeremy"
Best Rap Video	Arrested Development, "People Everyday"
Best Dance Video	En Vogue, "Free Your Mind"
Best Metal/ Hard Rock Video	Pearl Jam, "Jeremy"
Best Alternative Music Video	Nirvana, "In Bloom"
Best New Artist	Stone Temple Pilots, "Plush"
Breakthrough Video	Los Lobos, "Kiko and the Lavender Moon"
Viewer's Choice	Aerosmith, "Livin' on the Edge"
Best R & B Video	En Vogue, "Free Your Mind"

KURT LODER I think the best thing about the Video Music Awards is it's not really an awards show. No one cares who gets what award. No one cares. Who would care about this stuff? No one cares what position you came in, or the name of the award that you won, but the performances are always great. It's just a great concert. A wonderful, wonderful concert. It's the best awards show I know. And not only because I work here but because I honestly and sincerely mean it.

TRACI JORDAN Dr. Dre and Snoop Doggy Dogg were presenters for the awards show. They did their stint, did great. Dre had to do something else later in the show. I put Snoop in a trailer, got him some Kentucky Fried Chicken, some gin and juice, some video games, and he was very happy.

I have my headset on and Joel Gallen, head of production, calls me. "We've got a big problem. The LAPD and the sheriff's department are combing the audience looking for Snoop Doggy Dogg. They're here to arrest him." I immediately turn around, run into the audience, find Suge Knight, president of Death Row and Snoop's manager. "Go and get the car, we've gotta get Snoop out of here because the sheriff's here." He runs off. I run back to the trailer, open the door. The smoke comes billowing out like something out of a Cheech and Chong movie. Snoop's chilling on the couch. He's like, "Yo, T, is it time to go?" I'm like, "Yeah, it's time to go. The sheriff is here looking for you," and he's like, "What?"

Suge pulls up in the drop-top hydraulic car bouncing up and down like from the "Let Me Ride" video. I get Snoop downstairs and he turns around and he's like, "Yo Tray, you gotta go back in there, you gotta get my Converse gear," 'cuz they had sent him this huge duffel bag of stuff.

I go back in the trailer, I find the duffel bag, throw it over my shoulder. I'm going down the steps, and just at that point, Whoopi Goldberg is standing there. She's like, "Traci, what are you doing? I thought you had a big-time job here. Aren't you a vice president or something?"

Later I turn on the TV. And Snoop had apparently turned himself in on suspicion-of-murder charges. He was later acquitted. I am so glad he didn't get arrested backstage at the VMAs because that would have been the headline in the *L.A. Times* the next day.

KURT LODER Milton Berle somehow had trouble getting backstage. He was walking around with a towel over his head, being escorted by someone. Somebody stopped him at a gate and said, "Do you have your credential?" And Milton whips the towel off and says, "My face is my credential!" The guy went, "Whoa! OK!" Sort of the old Hollywood.

Chris Connelly

1988–present

KURT LODER Chris Connelly is another *Rolling Stone* refugee. He went on from *Rolling Stone* to work at *Premiere* magazine and then took a stand on a matter of principle there and quit. Very brave of him. Now he's a seasoned newsperson—*and* he speaks Latin.

CHRIS CONNELLY People always ask me, "Was it hard to make the transition from print to television?" I always said it was very hard for the people who had to watch me. For me it was a lot of fun. I just think it was difficult on the audience. I was kind of a ham and I had done a lot of TV. I'd been on *Oprah*, I'd done *Donahue*. I wasn't a total naif in terms of doing TV, although I kept saying I was. I'm sure that the people like Debbie Liebling, who had to work with me then, had a much more acute sense of my weaknesses than I did at the time. My appearance was certainly a challenge.

DEBBIE LIEBLING, former executive I had decided that Chris Connelly was the right person to host this movie show. I had hired him to do a little segment on a year-end movie wrapup. He was young, really knowledgeable, and had a great sense of humor.

Chris was a little awkward in his early days on television. He would come into my office after a taping, we would look at the tapes, and I would try as politely as I could to point out perhaps some areas that he could focus on. Chris took a few lessons, and he grew comfortable on camera very quickly. The great thing about Chris was that the talent just loved him.

CHRIS CONNELLY The 1997 Oscars®: I had been the editor of *Premiere* magazine for a while. I always worked at *Premiere* throughout my MTV career, and then I became the editor in chief, and then I left. Quentin Tarantino was under the impression that I had been the editor in charge when a piece that was about his natural father had run in the magazine, but I had never read it. I was gone by that time, but maybe my name was still on the masthead when the piece ran. Quentin, unbeknownst to me, found this a huge breach of something. So, it's March 1997—the piece ran in July 1996—and I'm out there for MTV waving my little mic cube, and I see him coming with Mira Sorvino, and I go, "Mira, hi, how are you?" She says, "Hi" and then Quentin, who'd apparently had a couple of bottles of Cristal in the limo ride over, grabs her by the neck and says, "That's the guy who did the thing about my dad."

And I go, "Nope, that wasn't me." And he sticks up his middle finger and mouths the words "fuck you." It looks like he's going to punch me. And I, who have never in my life had a fistfight, thought, great, my first fistfight and it's going to be on the red carpet going into the Oscars® in front of two thousand people and the entire world media. I wasn't scared, it was just like, *oh here we go*, and then he changes his mind at the last minute and decides to spit at me. But his aim was off and he didn't land any on me.

So he walks off and I turn to the camera and go, "Well, here comes Geoffrey Rush from *Shine*." Given my personality, I would have been much more rattled and upset if Tarantino had gotten right in my face and yelled at me for two minutes. But as it was, it was like living in New York.

Tabitha Soren

1990–97

DAVE SIRULNICK Tabitha was an intern with me when I worked at CNN. This eighteen-year-old rock 'n'-roll-loving girl, with big rock 'n' roll hair... If you look closely in the Beastie Boys "(You Gotta) Fight for Your Right (to Party)" video, she's in there, in the party scene. If you look closely, Tabitha is in there, in her early incarnation.

TABITHA SOREN The Beastie Boys have always had ultracool friends. Back during the "Fight for Your Right" video, they hung out with models. Somehow, I ended up in the middle of it, although I wasn't one of their friends. I ended up without pie in my hair, which was really important to me.

DAVE SIRULNICK Tabitha comes over to MTV. She starts as a writer. She's definitely on the metal tip. She does the first interview we ever did with Axl Rose, for *MTV News*. Nobody particularly wanted to do it. Tabitha says, "I'll go do it." She goes and does a great interview with Axl Rose. Anyway, she works for us for awhile and then goes away because she wants to pursue a career in television.

KURT LODER She went off to Vermont and just taught herself television. One of those deals where you would have to go out, operate the camera yourself, write the script yourself, stand up, do the read, pack the camera up, go back. She learned everything about television. So when she showed up, she was very presentable, and cute, and smart. It was great for the channel because she was interested in almost the opposite of everything I was interested in. I could be the remote curmudgeon, where she could be the happy smart girl over here. I think it worked out pretty well. We love Tabitha.

TABITHA SOREN I trained to be a reporter. I went to journalism school, studied political science. I had a very traditional news background. I worked at ABC *World News Tonight*, NBC, CNN. Reporters, with the exception of maybe ten people, don't get famous and are not in it for the glory.

JUDY MCGRATH, president, MTV group and chairman interactive music I remember Tabitha calling me at midnight from New Hampshire in '92 saying two things: "Pat Robertson asked me what MTV was, never heard of it ..." and "This guy Bill Clinton saw the MTV mic cube and got off the bus to talk to us." Tabitha and two interns with a camera fought through the Washington press pool and got us in the story.

She really did it; she was well-prepared and she changed the way politicians deal with anyone under 40. I'm a big fan.

JONATHAN ALTER, *Newsweek* magazine correspondent Tabitha became a star as a result of her political coverage. She would go up to New Hampshire or hold these town meetings, and she'd ask the questions that the viewer was wondering about but all of the old-fashioned political reporters didn't ask. She would cut through a lot of the crap and get to the central questions. Maybe the question would sound a little bit naive to old-fashioned political reporters, but that was actually better because it was closer to what the viewer wanted.

TABITHA SOREN "Choose or Lose" changed my life in that it established my work at a very young age as a serious reporter.

"Choose or Lose" changed my life personally because I met my husband [writer Michael Lewis] on the "Choose or Lose" bus in Seattle. He was there to do a story about young people and politics and extensively make fun of young people in the New Republic, and I was there to try to get him to take young people seriously. I don't think I have succeeded.

John Norris

1988–present

DEBBIE LIEBLING When I first started at MTV, John was a writer and he was writing the *Top 20 Countdown*. He was incredibly quiet, and he would just be sort of stowed away in a windowless office. It was kind of dark in there with just the light of his computer screen guiding him. And he would emerge every few days with the script. I remember being sort of surprised that his aspirations were to be on camera.

KURT LODER John is sort of on the dance beat. If something is going to happen in club news or something, he's around, he's a club guy, he can go out all night. He lives around where I live in New York, and I'm always anticipating seeing him if I'm walking out at eight in the morning. I'm always anticipating I'll see John just coming home.

JOHN NORRIS Kurt had been hired as the news anchor. And they knew that they were going to need an alternate. So the news director at the time asked me if I was interested in trying out and I was.

I don't think a lot of people remember the fact that I VJ'd. Which is OK with me, I am happy being associated with *MTV News*. I was on camera with *MTV News* from '88 to '91; '91 to '94 I was a VJ, and then came back to *News*. It was a bit different. What I did in terms of interviews wasn't all that different, it was just more studio-based things. One of the most challenging things about being a VJ is coming up with something new to say about a video that you've introduced about twenty times before.

20 Questions for 20 Years

DENIS LEARY

What song best describes your current state of mind?	"Asshole"
What is favorite video of all time?	Tonya Harding's "wedding night" video
What is your first memory of MTV?	Michael Jackson (original nose)
Where were you the first time you saw yourself on MTV and how did you react?	In prison. I said, "See? *That's* me. I can't be the killer."
Does the video enhance or hinder the song?	Yes
What is the most memorable moment you've witnessed on MTV?	Me at the VMA's with Cindy Crawford
Whose video work do you most admire?	Chuck Berry
What do you like most about MTV?	The music
What do you like least about MTV?	The music
What is your favorite guilty pleasure video?	Pamela and Tommy Lee
What do you consider to be MTV's greatest achievement and/or greatest failure in its first twenty years?	Downtown Julie Brown
What is the worst reaction you've received to one of your videos?	My 5-year-old son's teacher complaining that he taught "asshole" to all of his kindergarten classmates.
Videos should...	All star me
The best band name	The asshole band
The greatest moment in Rock and Pop and Rap was...	The bass player for Nirvana hitting me in the head with his guitar at the VMAs.
My biggest influence	George W. Bush
My favorite VMA performance	Howard Stern as "Fartman"
If I were president of MTV I would...	Force all acts to work in the nude.
What artist would you most like to work with and what would you like to do with them?	Porn films with Britney Spears.
Did video kill the radio star?	No. Throat cancer killed the radio star.
Special extra bonus:	Ted Demme sucks.

Randee of the Redwoods

DAVID FELTON, *Randee* **writer** Jim Turner did this character, Randee of the Redwoods, who was kind of an acid burnout, but a very lovable character. He had been doing it for years. The twentieth anniversary of the summer of love came around, '86 or '87, we did some promos with Randee. We did twenty in one weekend. A lot of them were just rewrites of what he did in his act and just put MTV in the line. He sort of caught on as a character on MTV.

JIM TURNER, *Randee* He was just a burned-out folk singer who couldn't complete a song, couldn't make a chord on his guitar. He was based on Barry Melton, who was the bass player for Country Joe and the Fish.

DAVID FELTON I love writing for characters who are kind of brain damaged because it really allows you to take leaps of logic. In '88 we decided to run Randee for president. We went down to Daytona and just had him announce his candidacy in front of this huge spring break crowd.

JIM TURNER Randee was just trying to figure out what the heck he was gonna do. Who his running mate was gonna be. The running mate ended up being this doll that we found when we went down to Daytona Beach at a junk store. I found this doll made out of half a doll's head and a bottle of Ivory liquid soap filled with sand. They had a weird robe over it. We called her Joan of Arc. She comes and speaks to me, "Randee, here is what you must do."

DAVID FELTON He didn't win and the country is the poorer for it, of course.

senator bob dole
republican presidential candidate, 1988

RANDEE

Woodstock '99

COVERAGE July 23–25
ATTENDANCE 225,000
LOCATION Rome, New York
OPENING ACT James Brown
CLOSING ACT Red Hot Chili Peppers

ANTHONY KIEDIS Anytime you get that many people together, you're gonna have the good, the bad, and the ugly.

CARSON DALY First of all, Woodstock was rad. The first two days I was there were awesome.

ANANDA LEWIS James Brown tripped me out. He opened the first day and had young folks headbanging to "Livin' in America." Kids were slam-dancing and body-surfing.

CARSON DALY But it got ugly, it went south quick. It's a concrete mess in the middle of what feels like a desert. There is no support, there's no shade. They're selling water, so people were pissed off.

BILLY JOE Particular members of some particular bands were trying to instigate something. What happened in '99 was complete bullshit. Of course, they were pissed off for a lot of reasons, but certain band members were getting off on it, and it's kinda like, "Come on, man, what are you doing?"

ANANDA LEWIS We were doing live Woodstock news. I think we might have done a few *TRL* hits but that was all over once the homebase started getting bombed with piss bottles.

CARSON DALY And the two hundred and fifty thousand people who were there, who were willing to sleep in mud, rain, and shit, aren't the same audience that sits home and writes letters to MTV— *Oh we love you Carson, we love* TRL—they're just not the same audience. So that was dangerous. They saw the *MTV News* cube go up there and it was like target practice. They were like, "Get out of here, we drove from Canada to see Tragically Hip."

ANANDA LEWIS Unfortunately, really, it was all directed toward Carson. There were a lot of guys in the audience and guys tend to playa-hate each other a little more. I know Carson's really popular and cute and at the time was dating Jennifer probably. So they were all mad at him. Maybe that's what it was all about. I'm not really sure.

CARSON DALY It was just open season. I was up there trying to do *TRL* live. And *TRL* has this teen image that aggro-testosterone frat guys just hate. So they're screaming, "Get off, fuck you, Backstreet Boys suck," the whole nine yards. I got hit with everything,

with bottles, cans, lipstick, any form of makeup. We put up a net—as if *that* was going to help. A watermelon was thrown up that broke the net.

ANTHONY KIEDIS Jimi Hendrix's sister knocked on our dressing room door five minutes before we're supposed to play. She said, "Could you play a song of my brother's?" because the whole Jimi Hendrix tribute that was supposed to happen fell apart at the last minute. The only one we could really remember how to play right was "Fire." As we went out for the encore, there were these beautiful columns of fire and the sky was just glorious and it was just a weird coincidence that we played "Fire."

ANANDA LEWIS The fires and being stuck on the bus on the way out, that was crazy, and Serena jumps off of the bus with a DV cam and goes out and does news segments in the middle of this shit. I'm like, whoa, but I guess if I had one, I would have done that too because that was the moment to catch, that's where the action is and that's where we should be. I didn't want to leave. I was ready to stay and they were like, "No this could get really serious." I never felt the threat, and that's just probably my own naivete.

CARSON DALY I sort of became the laughingstock of Woodstock because of the mud that people were throwing. It wasn't mud. It was the Porta-Potties pushed over. It was like shit water. It was disgusting. People were swimming in it. They were taking chunks of this mud and throwing it at me.

So I had cuts all over my arm from the day before from a Heineken bottle that was thrown at me. Now I'm thinking, *I have open wounds*, I mean I literally had cuts all down my arms. I'm not so hip to having this. I'm going to catch some disease. So I wore a blue ski jacket and it was a hundred degrees out and I'm on the air with it. I was doing it to protect my open wounds. That's how bad Woodstock was, it was like reporting from war.

STEVEN TYLER They threw up, they threw mud, they took too many drugs, they got sick, and they'll never forget it. For good or bad, at sixty and seventy they'll be talking to their friends. The only thing that bothered me was the corporate-in-your-face-overblown-it's-all-about-money. We already knew that.

JOE PERRY They really squeezed the life out of it commercially.

MARILYN MANSON People realized that it was just another T-shirt or another ticket to sell.

hey threw up, they threw mud, they took too many drugs, they got sick, and they'll never forget it.

"Choose or Lose"

TABITHA SOREN In the past, MTV did a lot of funny things. One of the things they did was have a candidate named Randee of the Redwoods who ran for president. This guy was hysterical. So MTV was doing something that I still think MTV does very well, which is put a funny spin on something very serious.

JIM TURNER, Randee of the Redwoods The day we went up to New Hampshire, there were ten inches of snow, just blizzarding. We drove around the state, we interviewed Al Haig, Bob Dole, it just blew my mind that these people would talk to us—and I was dressed like Randee. I asked Bob Dole his astrological sign and he goes, "Actually, I am a cusp."

Then we were somewhere at a big rally and I guess it was one of the debates and there were just hundreds of people outside and everybody was protesting something. One of the guys on the crew came over and said, "Hey there is a guy over here who is running for president, do you want to interview him?"

I had no idea who he was. So I said, "This is Randee at MTV and you're running for president. What is your name?"

"David Duke."

I'm thinking, *David Duke, who the hell is David Duke? I know that name, I know that name.* So I ask him, "Why are you running for president?" And he starts in on this thing about white people in this country just are getting an unfair shake and he handed us this pamphlet I still have to this day about the rough road white people have had to hoe in this country.

I was totally in character and that was the problem. If I was Jim and doing that, I would have tried to get in an argument. But I was trying to think, "What would be Randee's take on this?"

DAVE SIRULNICK 1992—We thought: the presidential election, let's jump in on it. People said we should do humor stuff, we should do another candidate like Randee, some said we should be flippant and not do it at all. And Tabitha was one of just a couple of people who thought we should do it serious. We really had no idea how the candidates would react.

TABITHA SOREN There were a lot of ideas about how we could make fun of the politicians, how we could make the political campaign entertaining because young people—it was assumed—weren't interested in the traditional type of news.

I went to the news director, Dave Sirulnick, and said that I would be interested in covering the campaign like what I considered a normal reporter. He thought that was a good idea. He felt like most of the coverage out there was very horse race–oriented and very dry and that if we were going to get our viewers' attention, we needed to do something different. And I said that I'd be that person.

Alison Stewart and I went up to New Hampshire by ourselves in the freezing cold in January. We didn't know how we were going to make it different . But once we started producing it, and Dave came up and gave us some much-needed direction, it sort of took the shape that eventually morphed into "Choose or Lose."

ALISON STEWART Tabitha and I were chasing around this big, chunky, red-faced governor of Arkansas named Bill Clinton. We finally cornered him in a library to do an interview.

TABITHA SOREN Day one with Clinton was actually in New Hampshire the day after the Gennifer Flowers story broke, so that day was very difficult. I had to

literally jump out of the bushes to interview him. I hid in the back of this library [where he was scheduled to appear] and Alison Stewart was in the front. We didn't know what entrance he was coming in and we had to be detectives and both be ready. Fortunately he came to my side and I had the cameraman as well. I got knocked in the head with the camera and I remember Clinton sort of patting my head and asking, "Are you OK?" 'cause I really got banged and there is footage of me hitting his hand away from my head. I was like, "Don't pat my head." I was defensive about seeming too young, I guess.

DAVE SIRULNICK Right at the beginning of the campaign we asked President George Bush to come on MTV. Bush makes some comment like, "I'm not going on some teenybopper network." Ross Perot was the other major candidate at this point, and we were going to do an interview with Ross Perot and then it was Clinton.

Clinton was trailing in the polls, he was in third place, and he was doing these town hall appearances.

So we booked a studio in Los Angeles and we brought in three hundred young people and we made it a big production and we made it a real big TV show. And that of course was the forum where he was face-to-face with young people and he was amazing with young people and he fed off of their energy.

That's where a young person stood up and asked him about gays in the military. A young woman stood up and asked what his position was on parental consent on abortions.

He talked about being the child of an alcoholic and he was baring himself to these young people. During every commercial break he'd go into the crowd and sit down with them and just talk with them. It was really huge for us. It put MTV's political coverage right on the map.

TABITHA SOREN President George Bush refused to talk to MTV the entire campaign. We talked to him on Halloween, which was three or four days before the election. He finally consented because his advisers had said, "Look, it's really close, you've got to try to do whatever you can to get more votes, so go ahead." We were on a train somewhere in the middle of Illinois I think, and he had gone into a meeting right

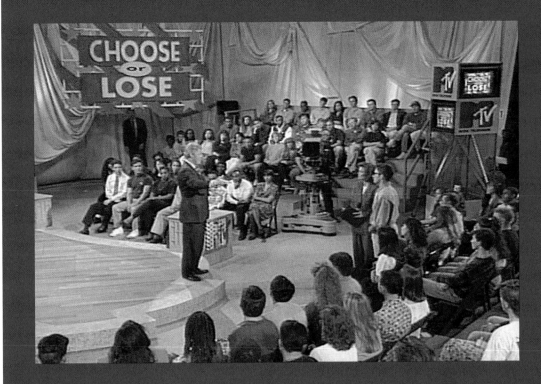

The Republican Convention

DAVE SIRULNICK Ted is a big supporter of the National Rifle Association. He's a big hunter and Ted was actually enjoying a little career resurgence at that time. So we're walking with him and because of Ted Nugent and MTV there was a number of press covering us and they're all sort of trailing behind us and they're all watching us. We get up to the gate, to the door, and as you can imagine, there's heavy security.

Ted stops and he looks at me and he says, "We've got a problem." I look at him and I say, "A problem?" And he says, "Yeah, we've got a problem." And I immediately realize what it is.

Ted's trying to get into the convention with a gun. So we run back to the *MTV News* office, he sits down, and it's not just a gun. It's an eight-inch hunting knife, you know, this big knife, in his pants! And in his boot, he's got a revolver. He unloads the revolver, unloads the knife, and I said, "Just keep this quiet and we'll go back out there." Ted's like, "Cool, no problem."

We walk back out there, we get back up and the press is like, "Where'd you go, what happened, what happened?" And his wife goes, "Oh, Ted just had to put his gun away." Needless to say, we had a lot of security going over every inch of Ted Nugent as we were walking around the convention.

before he did the interview with us and he found out that, basically, there was no chance of him winning. So this guy was not in a good mood.

DAVE SIRULNICK We get to this little car. They say, "Go outside and President Bush will come out in a second." And we're talking three feet, the little, little end of this train, a little balcony. We go out there, we're going forty m.p.h. down the tracks, it's windy, it's loud as all hell, Tabitha's ready, President Bush comes out. He's wearing his windbreaker, he's got a cup of coffee in his hand and a donut, and he had just come from breakfast. And his attitude was cavalier, "I don't care, I'm really not going to take this seriously." And Tabitha is hitting him with all the questions we had been asking, had been waiting to ask him all year.

TABITHA SOREN The funny thing was, President Bush was difficult during the interview. At the time I wasn't aware why. But afterward he signed a baseball for my dad and he started talking to me

about my father being in the military. He was so congenial. Usually, it's the exact opposite, politicians pretend to be sweet and charming while the camera is rolling and after the fact they're a jerk—certainly with celebrities that is the case.

KYLE MILLAR The "Choose or Lose" bus was pulled over a couple of times. One time that stands out in my mind was in Iowa. We got pulled over just for being the "Choose or Lose" bus. We weren't speeding. We weren't doing anything erratic. The cops pulled us over, wanted to just see what the inside of the bus looked like. And I think we gave them a couple of T-shirts and they went away and said everything was fine.

Inaugural Ball

DAVE SIRULNICK Bill Clinton becomes President Clinton, he wins. Very exciting time. Fast-forward, it's January 1993. When a president gets inaugurated, a lot of different states have balls, and a lot of other people have balls and because of "Choose or Lose," and the success we had as far as programming, we decided to throw *MTV's Inaugural Ball*.

It became the hottest ticket in town. Celebrities, Jack Nicholson, Billy Crystal. Everybody's flying in from Los Angeles to come to this thing. Every band wants to come to this thing. R.E.M. and U2 get together as Automatic Baby to do a song for that night. Soul Asylum performs. Boyz II Men performs. Everybody who was anybody wants in to the *MTV Ball*.

JUDY MCGRATH, president, MTV group and chairman interactive music We were next door to the official Arkansas Ball, and I remember thinking, as usual, *what if nobody cares?* Then Robert De Niro walks into our big empty ballroom and he heads straight for En Vogue's trailer. Later that night, everybody's trying to meet the Gore daughters.

CHRIS CONNELLY It was great. There was Natalie Merchant and Michael Stipe singing "To Sir with Love," which was amazing. Al Gore came out with Tipper and they looked like they were really enjoying the evening.

DENNIS MILLER I hosted the inaugural ball. I don't want to get too melodramatic, but it's a pretty electric feeling because you realize a great portion of the world's youth is watching you.

DAVE SIRULNICK President Clinton, of course, has a choice of a hundred things to do that night, and we hear that he's going to come to our ball. We're very excited. We're on the air for thirty seconds when we heard the announcement in the production truck that President Clinton's here, he's going to be on the stage in about a minute.

TABITHA SOREN The President and Hillary Rodham Clinton showed up early. The prompter was still typing because they couldn't figure out whether to call her Hillary Rodham Clinton or Hillary Clinton. I just had to wing it and that was nerve-racking.

DENNIS MILLER Just as I was doing my monologue, I just remember like seventy-four flags; I felt one of those laser rifle sights on my head, but there was no choice about me not getting offstage. I think I stopped in the middle of a word.

TABITHA SOREN It was like, "Tabitha you have your shoes on, get out there." Seriously, I remember the makeup woman was after me about lipstick. It was a very last-minute thing.

DAVE SIRULNICK Dennis Miller's vamping, he tosses it to Tabitha and Tabitha says, "Ladies and gentlemen, the President of the United States and the first lady." And he comes out.

PRESIDENT BILL CLINTON I think everybody knows that MTV had a lot to do with the Clinton-Gore victory.

DAVE SIRULNICK And in the truck, the president of our company, Judy McGrath, falls over. She just couldn't believe it. Nobody believed it, that the President of the United States is thanking this rock 'n' roll network that's home of *Beavis and Butt-Head* for helping him get elected.

TOM FRESTON I remember turning around and everyone was giving high-fives to each other. They said, "I can't believe this is true. How did we stumble into this?"

NATALIE MERCHANT It's the first time I've ever been moved to happiness because of government. It was a ball for the youth vote. For years we have heard about of the apathy of the youth of America. We showed them that when we are given a choice we are excited and vote.

PETER JENNINGS I think it says a lot about the MTV audience that the MTV Inaugural Ball was the President's first stop of the night.

TABITHA SOREN I thought Aerosmith was the greatest band in the world when I was in high school. Every time I interview them, I get transported back in time, and I'm sixteen years old again, big hair, wearing a headband, and I feel really ridiculous. But Joe Perry and Steven Tyler are both very smart people, they're very articulate, and they're so media-savvy that they're a great interview.

So when I asked Steven Tyler about the rumors about him doing drugs during the recording of their record, he threatened to do a urine test right then and there. I thought, *I don't really want to see that.* It was right after Michael Stipe showed me the scar from his appendix surgery, and he had to basically pull down his pants a little farther than I needed to see—too much information. I thought I was gonna have a repeat, and really, that was enough skin for one show. I said I'd take his word for it.

VMA 1994

DATE September 8
LOCATION Radio City Music Hall, New York
HOST Roseanne

PERFORMERS

Aerosmith	"Walk This Way"
Beastie Boys	"Sabotage"
Bruce Springsteen	"Streets of Philadelphia"
Green Day	"Basketcase"
Rolling Stones	"Love Is Strong" and "Start Me Up"
Salt-n-Pepa	"Shoop"/"Whatta Man"/ "None of Your Business"
Smashing Pumpkins	"Disarm"
Leningrad Cowboys and the Alexander Red Army Ensemble	"Sweet Home Alabama"
Stone Temple Pilots	"Pretty Penny"
Snoop Doggy Dogg	"Murder Was the Case"
Tom Petty and the Heartbreakers	"Mary Jane's Last Dance"
Boyz II Men	"I'll Make Love to You"

WINNERS

Best Video	Aerosmith, "Cryin"
Best Male Video	Tom Petty and the Heartbreakers, "Mary Jane's Last Dance"
Best Female Video	Janet Jackson, "If"
Best Group Video	Aerosmith, "Cryin"
Best Rap Video	Snoop Doggy Dogg, "Doggy Dogg World"
Best Dance Video	Salt-n-Pepa featuring En Vogue, "Whatta Man"
Best Metal/ Hard Rock Video	Soundgarden, "Black Hole Sun"
Best Alternative Music Video	Nirvana, "Heart-Shaped Box"
Best New Artist	Counting Crows, "Mr. Jones"
Breakthrough Video	R.E.M., "Everybody Hurts"
Michael Jackson's Video Vanguard	Tom Petty and the Heartbreakers
Viewer's Choice	Aerosmith, "Cryin'"

BILLY CORGAN I was out of my mind on way too many drugs. We were playing "Disarm," but we were doing a heavy version. I realized at that moment I was over the line. My guitar string broke and I ripped down the mic stand. When you're out of control on tour it seems very obvious. But when you're out of control in front of America you realize, "This is way too silly, I'm taking this way too seriously."

SNOOP DOGG I wanted to express something that was really on my heart. To let the public know that I was innocent and that I'm a musician and I've been wrongfully accused and I am innocent until proven guilty. This song was a way for me of venting that out. So we put together a proper little stage show, where we were not trying to disrespect or offend anybody, but it was just depicting what I had put on a record already. So when we did it, when we went through it in rehearsal, we felt it, so we put it on the VMA and it turned out to be a big success for me.

20 Questions for 20 Years

TABITHA SOREN
MTV NEWS 1991–1998

What song best describes your current state of mind?	"Smile," Jayhawks, "It's a Beautiful Day," U2
What is favorite video of all time?	Liz Phair, "Supernova," Yo La Tengo, "Tom Courtenay"
What is your first memory of MTV?	Students from our junior high school in Florida petitioning our local cable company to keep MTV on the air, after protests by religious groups.
Where were you the first time you saw yourself on MTV and how did you react?	Former MTV news reporter Tad Low talked me into watching both our debuts at a sports bar on a TV screen so huge you could count the pores in our faces.
Does the video enhance or hinder the song?	A good video provides even an annoying song (i.e. Blind Melon's "No Rain") (The Bee Girl).
What is the most memorable moment you've witnessed on MTV?	Public Enemy's Chuck D interviewing Sen. Strom Thurmond CR-SC) at the '96 Republican Convention.
Whose video work do you most admire?	Spike Jonze, Madonna
What do you like most about MTV?	Its irreverent attitude toward the straight world as well as its viewers and artists.
What do you like least about MTV?	Its lack of interest in bands without a major label behind them.
What is your favorite guilty pleasure video?	Nine Inch Nails, "Enema," Lisa Loeb, "I Do," "Stay"
What do you consider to be MTV's greatest achievement and/or greatest failure in its first 20 years?	Only rarely in the past 20 years has MTV managed to distinguish its music playlist from radio's. That is a waste. So much great music is ignored.
What is the worst reaction you've received to one of your videos?	After listening to me interview young voters, my husband thought their comments were so uninformed, that their right to vote should be revoked.
Videos should . . .	Enable fans who can't afford concert tickets a chance to see their favorite bands perform.
The best band name	KISS, The Breeders, Belly, Nirvana
The greatest moment in Rock and Pop and Rap was	Lisa Marie Presley marrying Michael Jackson.
My biggest influence	Currently, my two-year-old daughter Quinn Tallulah
My favorite VMA performance	Courtney Love humiliating herself in front of Madonna postshow '94.
If I were President of MTV I would . . .	Devote more airtime to political issues and somehow convince G. W. Bush to start a dialogue with young voters.
What artist would you most like to work with and what would you like to do with them?	R.E.M., Tom Petty and the Heartbreakers, Sheryl Crow, Billy Corgan—because they were self-aware, articulate, and had their hearts in the right place.
Did video kill the radio star?	Only the really ugly ones.

Matt Pinfield

1995–2000

MATT PINFIELD I was a real music fan. I met a lot of people at MTV who worked here in the music department who listened to my radio station. They lived on the Jersey shore or they lived in lower Manhattan. When I found out that Dave Kendall had left *120 Minutes*, I just asked, "You guys looking for a host?"

At the time there were not a lot of bald guys on television. The bald thing hadn't really broken through yet. I remember them saying, "I don't think your look or your age is right but we'll get back to you."

They called and said, "We're thinking of giving you a shot 'cause Oasis is coming in. You're a fan of theirs." Oasis of course had the reputation of being really hard to deal with and not wanting to be cooperative. People are going to me, "Oh man, what a tough one, what a one to throw you in on." I'm like, "I love Oasis." I came in with Oasis. Afterward, the MTV people came up to me and said, "Matt, I thought you did a great job, man. We'd like to sign you onto the show right away."

Now I look and Ben Stiller's doing imitations of me. This is just insane. Ben Stiller had to go through two-and-a-half hours of makeup to try and look like me. I was just in shock when I saw it. Some people were like, "Wow, are you kinda pissed? He was busting your chops real hard." No man, it's cool. That is what comedy is.

I was flattered. I met him. He told me, "Matt, it would have been great if we could have done dueling Matts."

PREMIERE March 10, 1986
FINALE May 8, 2000
MTV's longest running show
HOSTS Alan Hunter, J. J. Jackson, Kevin Seal, Dave Kendall, Lewis Largent, and Matt Pinfield

FIRST FOUR VIDEOS TO AIR ON SHOW The Cure's "Close to Me," 10,000 Maniacs' "Scorpio Rising," PiL's "Rise," Clannad's "In a Lifetime"

VIDEOS THAT MADE THEIR DEBUTS ON 120 MINUTES Nirvana's "Smells Like Teen Spirit," Pixies' "Here Comes Your Man," R.E.M.'s "The One I Love"

ANTHONY KIEDIS It was comedy to me. I loved *120 Minutes*. That was my show.

Pauly Shore

1990–95

PAULY SHORE It was '88. Me sitting at my mom's house, watching *Spring Break* and going, "I got to be there," 'cause I want to get laid. I threw away all my books, and focused on a plan: how to get laid at *Spring Break*. I knew if I was there and I got on camera, then I would get laid.

DOUG HERZOG, former executive I knew Pauly's mother, Mitzi, who ran the Comedy Store. There was a woman who ran talent for us at the time named Drue Wilson and she was a big Pauly fan. Pauly was down at *Spring Break*. We didn't bring him down there. He was down there performing on his own. Drue was dragging him everywhere. He was following us around everywhere we went. We couldn't shake him. He was just so desperate to be on MTV.

PAULY SHORE I started developing my stand-up comedy. MTV was very East Coast. It was Adam Curry, it was Ken Ober. It was *Remote Control*, this kind of stiff New York thing. It was just very "in the studio." And I was from California. My hair was here. I was dressing like half-gay with my mom's stuff, and half like Steven Tyler. Drew Wilson brought me to *Spring Break*, Daytona '89.

It was me, Christian Slater, Adam Sandler, and Corey Feldman had all the girls. He had his Michael Jackson thing on with his white makeup on and his shades. Christian was there promoting *Gleaming the Cube*.

It was awful. I was very nervous. Remember when you were a kid, and you go to a new school? You feel very uncomfortable. That's how I felt, times ten. I didn't know how to talk to people. I still don't know how to talk to people.

Drue Wilson calls me and says, "Look lovey, we want you to come to host the Pepperdine half-hour comedy hour, but you're not going to be on camera." And I was like, okay, anything. Mario Joyner usually hosted it, but I came kicking out. I thought I was all the man.

DOUG HERZOG We shot a comedy concert out here, called *Five Funny Guys*. He wasn't one of the five. He was the sixth funny guy, not for air, to warm up the crowd. We had the cameras rolling, and he killed.

They brought the tape back to me. They said, "You got to see Pauly Shore. Maybe we should try him out." And the next thing you know, it's *Totally Pauly*. No one knew quite what to make of it, but the audience seemed to like it. It certainly had its moment on MTV. There's no question about it, there was a Pauly era.

PAULY SHORE Did you ever have sex with anyone, and after you wake up in the morning, there's like a big mark in the sheet? That's how I feel. I feel I left my mark there at MTV.

My comedy persona, my stand-up persona, developed into the show. It was really an accident. It wasn't like I sat home and planned the whole pause in between words and the grindage. It was one of those things where I was on the show, and I was throwing to a video and I said, "Check out this video because its going to be ma-jor." A week or two after it aired, a kid came up to me and was like, "Man yo ma-jor." I was like, "What are you talking about?" And he goes, "Dude, that's you. You do 'ma-jor.'" I'm like, "Okay, cool." I just started pausing in between all my wo-rds. Like th-at.

1993

Movie Awards

BEN STILLER It's just a lot of people running around having fun partying, partying down. It's a big party, man. It's a huge party.

RICK AUSTIN, producer, Movie Awards It has to be the anti-Oscars® because it's MTV. You can't take this seriously. It's not about films, it's about movies. It's really about what everybody likes to see when they go to a movie and they pay their money and eat their popcorn. When Dennis Miller came in as the first host, his attitude really informed a lot of what we did.

DENNIS MILLER I remember those were the most fun times I've had hosting an awards show. I just remember the MTV people were always the coolest and it was neat to see because when you watch it you think, "I hope I don't go to meet them and end up in some star chamber with a bunch of squares who do double-blind window tests in malls to figure out what's cool. I hope they're actually cool." And they are cool.

Movie Awards 1992

HOST Dennis Miller
VENUE Walt Disney Studios, Burbank, California
AWARD Purple film reel

PERFORMERS En Vogue, "My Love (You're Never Gonna Get It)," Ugly Kid Joe, "Everything About You," Arrested Development, "Tennessee," Vince Neil, "You're Invited (But Your Friend Can't Come)"

WINNERS

Best Movie	*Terminator 2: Judgment Day*
Best Male Performance	Arnold Schwarzenegger, *Terminator 2: Judgment Day*
Best Female Performance	Linda Hamilton, *Terminator 2: Judgment Day*
Breakthrough Performance	Edward Furlong, *Terminator 2: Judgment Day*
Best Onscreen Duo	Dana Carvey/Mike Myers, *Wayne's World*
Best Villain	Rebecca DeMornay, *The Hand That Rocks the Cradle*
Best Comedic Performance	Billy Crystal, *City Slickers*
Best Song	"(Everything I Do) I Do It for You," Bryan Adams (from *Robin Hood: Prince of Thieves*)
Best Kiss	Anna Chlumsky/Macauley Culkin, *My Girl*
Best New Filmmaker	John Singleton, *Boyz N the Hood*
Lifetime Achievement	Jason Voorhees, *Friday the Thirteenth*

RICK AUSTIN One of the biggest categories the first couple of years was Best Song because it's MTV. The first year Guns N' Roses and Bryan Adams and all these big acts at the time were nominated. The original idea was, "OK, we'll get 'em all to perform," but of course Guns N' Roses can't make it and Bryan Adams is in Canada. Chris Kreski, one of our writers, happened to be working with William Shatner. A few of us *Star Trek* geeks who worked on the show knew about Shatner's other career as a musical dramatist. We had his records where he interpreted "Mr. Tambourine Man." We thought, "Well, if we can't get the artists to perform, we must have Shatner." We did the Priceline idea like eight years before. Now there's a whole new generation of Shatnerites out there.

DENNIS MILLER I've been on board with Bill Shatner's interpretive talents for years. That's always genius.

CHRIS KRESKI, writer On the day of the shoot, Shatner was late. They called his house, called his agent, called his car phone, nothing. We were eating studio time with a whole bunch of musicians sitting around doing nothing, and we've got a star who's a no-show. Finally, Robin Berlin gets a phone call explaining what's happened. Shatner was out riding one of his horses that morning, and he fell off...onto his head. "Is he OK?" she asked. "Well, he's fine, but we think he has a concussion, he's pretty loopy...but he's coming to the shoot anyway."

Shatner shows up a few minutes later, clearly addled by falling on his head. He's silly, he says "hello" to me three different times as if he's just arrived, he's giggling, his eyes are glassy. We sort of push Shatner into the studio at this point, and he proceeds to absolutely *nail* the bits. He's brilliant. We're crying-laughing in the control room. I swear to you the concussion helped his performance—there's no way Shatner could have been that loopy were it not for the concussion.

1993

HOST Eddie Murphy
VENUE Walt Disney Studios, Burbank, California
AWARD Popcorn award makes its debut

PERFORMERS Village People, "In the Navy"/"Macho Man"/"YMCA," Duran Duran, "Ordinary World," Stone Temple Pilots, "Plush," Dr. Dre/Snoop Doggy Dogg, "Nothin but a G Thang," Rod Stewart, "Have I Told You Lately"

WINNERS

Best Movie	*A Few Good Men*
Best Male Performance	Denzel Washington, *Malcolm X*
Best Female Performance	Sharon Stone, *Basic Instinct*
Breakthrough Performance	Marisa Tomei, *My Cousin Vinny*
Best Onscreen Duo	Mel Gibson/Danny Glover, *Lethal Weapon 3*
Best Villain	Jennifer Jason Leigh, *Single White Female*
Best Comedic Performance	Robin Williams, *Aladdin*
Best Song	"I Will Always Love You," Whitney Houston (from *The Bodyguard*)
Best Kiss	Marisa Tomei/Christian Slater, *Untamed Heart*
Best New Filmmaker	Carl Franklin, *One False Move*
Lifetime Achievement	The Three Stooges

VAN TOFFLER, president, MTV and MTV2 Jim Carrey's manager didn't even know who he was at first. It was very impressive. Jim came over to us while we were talking. And Courtney Love had no idea who he was when he got up to kiss her. She realized it while he was onstage and he started talking about her. She had just shot a movie with him.

1999

1994

HOST Will Smith

VENUE Sony Studios, Culver City, California

PERFORMERS Bon Jovi, "Good Guys Don't Always Wear White," John Mellencamp/Me'Shell NdegéOcello, "Wild Night," Dave Carpenter, David Goldbath, Toby Huss, and John Prophet do Best Song Medley, *Backbeat* band: Greg Dulli, Don Fleming, Dave Grohl, Mike Mills, Thurston Moore, and Dave Pirner "Money (That's What I Want)"/"Long Tall Sally"/"Helter Skelter"

WINNERS

Best Movie	*Menace II Society*
Best Male Performance	Tom Hanks, *Philadelphia*
Best Female Performance	Janet Jackson, *Poetic Justice*
Breakthrough Performance	William Baldwin, *Silver*
Best Onscreen Duo	Harrison Ford/Tommy Lee Jones, *The Fugitive*
Best Villain	Alicia Silverstone, *The Crush*
Best Comedic Performance	Robin Williams, *Mrs. Doubtfire*
Best Song	"Will You Be There," Michael Jackson (from *Free Willy*)
Best Kiss	Demi Moore/Woody Harrelson, *Indecent Proposal*
Best New Filmmaker	Steven Zaillian, *Searching for Bobby Fischer*
Lifetime Achievement	Richard Roundtree, *Shaft*

LEONARD MALTIN My favorite MTV parody was the one for *Basic Instinct*. If you haven't got the lighting just right, if you haven't got the atmosphere and the set close enough, and most importantly if you haven't got the actors in the right frame of mind, if they're not approaching it the right way, it's not going to come off. Florence Henderson is a Broadway-trained actress of many years experience. Even though everyone knows her mostly as Mrs. Brady, she's no lightweight. She knew how to pull that off and she's terrific at it. What makes it work is that she is so into it; she's not winking at the audience, she's taking it seriously. The best parodies are the ones where the people in those roles take them seriously and do it right.

JOEL GALLEN, producer Initially Florence thought it was funny but she needed some positive reinforcement. She needed somebody else to convince her that this was a good idea. So I called the guy that created *The Brady Bunch*, Sherwood Schwartz. I sent him the scripts. He thought they were hilarious, called Florence and after she got the assurance from Sherwood that it was a cool thing to do, not only did she do it, she got into it.

1993

1995

CHRIS KRESKI We reenacted the famous leg-crossing scene. We put Florence Henderson in the white Sharon Stone dress, and had the Brady kids "interrogate" her. We wrote the piece *very* close to the original script, but added Brady-isms wherever they'd fit. Instead of "cocaine," the coffee-swilling Carol Brady sings the praises of "fucking on caffeine." She talks about how she'd had sex with Sam the Butcher, and how she tied him up. It was hard to listen to Mrs. Brady talk like a big slut, but it was also really funny. We buttoned the piece in a really good way too. Instead of going for the obvious crossing-of-the-legs gag, we had Mrs. Brady raise her hands behind her head, exposing a huge tuft of pit hair. It was a *great* sight gag, and it brought screams from the house. It was a great feeling.

FLORENCE HENDERSON Hey, let's face it. Everybody in show business wants to be a part of the MTV Movie Awards. And for me I must say it's right up there with *The Brady Bunch* for memories for people. They still talk about the MTV Movie Awards and my appearance on it.

HOSTS Courteney Cox and Jon Lovitz
VENUE Warner Brothers Studios, Burbank, California

PERFORMERS Boyz II Men, "Water Runs Dry," Blues Traveler, "Runaround," TLC, "Waterfalls," the Ramones

WINNERS

Best Movie	*Pulp Fiction*
Best Male Performance	Brad Pitt, *Interview with the Vampire*
Best Female Performance	Sandra Bullock, *Speed*
Breakthrough Performance	Kirsten Dunst, *Interview with the Vampire*
Best Onscreen Duo	Sandra Bullock/ Keanu Reeves, *Speed*
Best Villain	Dennis Hopper, *Speed*
Best Comedic Performance	Jim Carrey, *The Mask*
Best Song	"Big Empty," Stone Temple Pilots (from *The Crow*)
Best Kiss	Lauren Holly/Jim Carrey, *Dumb and Dumber*
Best New Filmmaker	Steve James, *Hoop Dreams*
Lifetime Achievement	Jackie Chan

CHRIS KRESKI Arnold Schwarzenegger was presenting an award on the show, and we'd written six or eight possible bits for him, hoping he'd read them all and like at least one. We sent them out a few days before the show, and never heard back. Come show day, we hadn't heard anything. Arnold arrived for the show that afternoon, and I got a walkie-talkie call saying that I needed to go talk to him immediately. Right away I got a stomachache. No star ever calls for a writer with good news. They only yell for writers when they hate their lines. My best guess was that Arnold had just read what we'd sent him and despised everything. I headed for his dressing room feeling like I was going to barf.

When I got to Arnold's dressing room, Arnold was seated at a makeup table, smoking a cigar, and wearing the loudest Hawaiian shirt I'd ever seen. I was dying to ask him where he got it. However, knowing that he'd probably be yelling at me any second now, I held my tongue. Instead, as I watched him reading through his possible lines, I kept trying to read the manufacturer's tag sticking out of the shirt pocket. I could almost read it from where I was, but not quite. I leaned in closer, then closer again, all

1999

1999

1992

the while trying to look cool. At that point, without ever looking up, Arnold grabbed my forearm. My lower intestine did a backflip.

"Vatt are you doing?" Arnold asked.

"I'm sorry," I said, "but that's maybe the coolest shirt I've ever seen. I was trying to read the tag."

"Yahh, diss iss a gutt one," Arnold said.

"Sure is. Not many of us manly enough to pull this look off."

"Haaaaaaa." Arnold laughed way too loud, and hit me on the back, which hurt a lot. He then told me that he'd called for a writer because he actually liked three of the possible bits we'd sent over. He wanted to thank us for sending over so many possibilities. He also wanted feedback as to which of the three bits I thought would get him the biggest laugh. That was cool. He even gave me a cigar.

1996

HOST Janeane Garofalo and Ben Stiller
VENUE Walt Disney Studios, Burbank, California

PERFORMERS Whitney Houston, "Why Does It Hurt So Bad," Garbage, "Only Happy When It Rains," Fugees (with Roberta Flack), "Killing Me Softly," Adam Sandler, "Mel Gibson"

WINNERS
Best Movie	*Seven*
Best Male Performance	Jim Carrey, *Ace Ventura 2: When Nature Calls*
Best Female Performance	Alicia Silverstone, *Clueless*
Breakthrough Performance	George Clooney, *From Dusk Till Dawn*
Best Onscreen Duo	Chris Farley/David Spade, *Tommy Boy*
Best Villain	Kevin Spacey, *Seven*
Best Comedic Performance	Jim Carrey, *Ace Ventura 2: When Nature Calls*
Best Song	"Sittin' Up in My Room," Brandy (from *Waiting to Exhale*)
Best Kiss	Natasha Henstridge/Anthony Guidera, *Species*
Best New Filmmaker	Wes Anderson, *Bottle Rocket*
Lifetime Achievement	Godzilla

HEATHER PARRY Producing the 1999 preshow with Bijou Phillips was like another night on the town for her. It was just her saying "hi" to her friends, and her running around. She was a little hard to control for the producer that was working with her. I'd say, "OK, I'm ready for Bijou," and she'd be in the wide shot just running up and down the carpet. But the one thing that Bijou did do, which was hysterical, because she's just blunt, is she was interviewing Mike Myers.

1992

They were chatting politely before we started rolling. He says, "I can't be out in the sun, I'm a redhead." And she's like, "You're a redhead?" 'Cause Mike Myers is standing there with brown hair. "You're not a redhead." He says, "No, no. I'm a redhead." And they go, "Three, two, one" to do the segment, and she's like, "OK! I'm here with Firecrotch." And Mike Myers was just sort of like, "Ellleeugh."

1999

1999

1997

HOST Mike Myers
VENUE Barker Hangar, Santa Monica, California
HIGHLIGHTS Mike Myers opens the show with his "Lord of the Dance" routine. *TV Guide* calls it the "funniest moment in the history of television."
PERFORMERS Bush, "Cold Contagious," Jewel, "Foolish Games," En Vogue, "Whatever," Ming Tea, "BBC."

WINNERS

Best Movie	*Scream*
Best Male Performance	Tom Cruise, *Jerry Maguire*
Best Female Performance	Claire Danes, *William Shakespeare's Romeo and Juliet*
Breakthrough Performance	Matthew McConaughey, *A Time to Kill*
Best Onscreen Duo	Nicolas Cage/Sean Connery, *The Rock*
Best Villain	Jim Carrey, *The Cable Guy*
Best Comedic Performance	Jim Carrey, *The Cable Guy*
Best Song	"Machinehead," Bush (from *Fear*)
Best Kiss	Vivica A. Fox/Will Smith, *Independence Day*
Best Fight	Fairuza Balk/Robin Tunney, *The Craft*
Best New Filmmaker	Doug Liman, *Swingers*
Lifetime Achievement	Chewbacca

CHRISTINA NORMAN, marketing and promotions executive Chris Rock sits right down and does the shot. It's just what you expect. He bitches a little about having to look like Rigoletto and then he's, "All right, I get it." We needed him to sit in this clown chair and put on these clown shoes. And there was something else they wanted him to wear, the three-cornered hat. He said, "No, you got your shoes, you're done. Take your picture."

Chris Rock is the easiest person in the world to work with. For that year's Video Music Awards we had a huge promo idea, which was basically a musical, like *West Side Story*. We pitched it to everybody else and they loved it. And then we pitched it to Chris, who said, "That sounds like it's going to take a long time. I don't have a long time. What else have you got?"

When you look at the talent we got for the opera shoot, it was everybody who was about to get huge: Britney, Eminem, Kid Rock—amazing talent, which is what made it so difficult for the next year. I've done a lot of VMA campaigns and every year after the show I'm like, "How the fuck are we going to top that next year?"

1997

1998

1994

2000

1998

HOST Samuel L. Jackson
VENUE Barker Hangar, Santa Monica, California
PERFORMERS The Wallflowers, "Heroes," Brandy and Mase, "Sittin' on Top of the World," Natalie Imbruglia, "Torn"

WINNERS

Best Movie	*Titanic*
Best Male Performance	Leonardo DiCaprio, *Titanic*
Best Female Performance	Neve Campbell, *Scream 2*
Breakthrough Performance	Heather Graham, *Boogie Nights*
Best Onscreen Duo	John Travolta/Nicolas Cage, *Face/Off*
Best Villain	Mike Myers, *Austin Powers: International Man of Mystery*
Best Comedic Performance	Jim Carrey, *Liar Liar*
Best Song	"Men in Black," Will Smith (from *Men in Black*)
Best Kiss	Adam Sandler/Drew Barrymore, *The Wedding Singer*
Best New Filmmaker	Peter Cattaneo, *The Full Monty*
Lifetime Achievement	Clint Howard

RICK AUSTIN The MTV Movie Awards, where music and Hollywood meet, is probably the only time you'll see Renee Zellweger and Jewel together in a room, because it could have been true that they are the same person. They look exactly alike and I think they realize that. I think they're actually friends now because they realize that they get mistaken for each other all the time. I actually saw a couple of people come up to Renee at the show and go "Jewel, you were so great."

JANEANE GAROFALO I love when they gave the lifetime achievement award to Ron Howard's brother, and they referred to him as Ron Howard's brother, which made me laugh so hard because that's how everyone knows him.

JIM CARREY Clint Howard's lifetime achievement award was so deserving. There's a soul that's lived, he's seen the darkness, he's seen the light and you just want to go with him. Clint takes you down a stream by a river and he feeds you tea and oranges that come all the way from the kitchen. He's amazing.

JUDY MCGRATH, president, MTV group and chairman interactive music I remember Tom Hanks hung out backstage after the show so that his kids could meet Michael Stipe and Courtney Love and all the music people. They were so into it, and I'm thinking, *You guys eat dinner with Steven Spielberg and you're impressed with this?* He struck me as a very good dad.

2000

1996

1999

HOST Lisa Kudrow
VENUE Barker Hangar, Santa Monica, California
PERFORMERS Will Smith featuring Dru Hill, Kool Moe Dee, and Stevie Wonder, "Wild Wild West," Kid Rock, "Bawitdaba," Robbie Williams, "Millennium"

WINNERS

Best Movie	*There's Something About Mary*
Best Male Performance	Jim Carrey, *The Truman Show*
Best Female Performance	Cameron Diaz, *There's Something About Mary*
Breakthrough Performance Male	James Van Der Beek, *Varsity Blues*
Breakthrough Performance Female	Katie Holmes, *Disturbing Behavior*
Best Onscreen Duo	Jackie Chan/Chris Tucker, *Rush Hour*
Best Villain	Matt Dillon, *There's Something About Mary*; Stephen Dorff, *Blade*
Best Comedic Performance	Adam Sandler, *The Waterboy*
Best Song	"I Don't Want to Miss a Thing," Aerosmith (from *Armageddon*)
Best Kiss	Gwyneth Paltrow/Joseph Fiennes, *Shakespeare in Love*

JOEL GALLEN In 1999, we wanted to do a *South Park* film 'cause the *South Park* movie was coming out. We were already planning a *Star Wars* parody with Andy Dick and Lisa Kudrow. *South Park* got down to the wire. They were very busy finishing their movie. They finally sent us their storyboards and their audio of the film that they wanted to do. It was a little bit of a slam to *Star Wars* and certainly to the Jar-Jar Binks character. We felt it was crossing the line, even on the MTV Movie Awards.

RICK AUSTIN A lot of people were criticizing Jar-Jar Binks as sort of being a computer-generated Stepin Fetchit racial stereotype of some kind. And of course *South Park* wants to take this Jar-Jar thing to its logical extreme. So they start making this *South Park* parody about Jar-Jar running loose in South Park as like the biggest racial stereotype you've ever seen. We realized that it would not be good for anybody for this thing to air. You don't want to alienate the audience, you don't want to alienate George Lucas.

2000

1999

1993

1993

1992

1999

2000

HOST Sarah Jessica Parker
VENUE Sony Pictures Studios, Culver City, California
PERFORMERS D'Angelo, "Devils Pie," *NSYNC, "It's Gonna Be Me," Metallica, "I Disappear"

WINNERS

Best Movie	*The Matrix*
Best Male Performance	Keanu Reeves, *The Matrix*
Best Female Performance	Sarah Michelle Gellar, *Cruel Intentions*
Breakthrough Performance Male	Haley Joel Osment, *The Sixth Sense*
Breakthrough Performance Female	Julia Stiles, *10 Things I Hate About You*
Best Onscreen Duo	Mike Myers/Verne Troyer, *Austin Powers: The Spy Who Shagged Me*
Best Villain	Mike Myers, *Austin Powers: The Spy Who Shagged Me*
Best Kiss	Sarah Michelle Gellar/ Selma Blair, *Cruel Intentions*
Best New Filmmaker	Spike Jonze, *Being John Malkovich*

ROBIN BERLIN, former executive Tom Hanks was nominated for Best Male Performance in *Philadelphia*. We were absolutely thrilled that he was there. We were thrilled that *anyone* was there. Anytime the nominees show up, you really want to roll out the red carpet. And his chair collapsed in the middle of the show. He was sitting there in a lovely theater chair and suddenly, as though it were made out of paper, it just collapsed and he was on the floor. We were all mortified but he was in a good humor about it.

RICK AUSTIN Jim Carrey is the king of the MTV Movie Awards. I think he always will be the king. If Michael Jackson is the King of Pop, Jim Carrey is the King of the MTV Movie Awards. I think he's won more movie awards than anybody.

ROBIN WILLIAMS The MTV Movie Awards just seems to be the Golden Globes® on acid. There is a lot more going on in the audience. You don't get a lot of that at the Oscars®. OHHHHHH Thalberg Award! You have to be careful, especially when Warren is speaking, not to operate heavy machinery. The Academy Awards® have a certain decorum but it was nice when I came out with 24 girls and gave a 24-bun salute.

1999

Daisy Fuentes

1990–98

DAISY FUENTES I was working for Univision, then for Telemundo, the two Latin stations. I had no clue what I was doing. I sucked at it. I had no idea why I lasted as long as I did.

I sent in a tape basically begging for an audition. I just sent a tape with my nasty, tacky, bad hair, Spanish TV weather footage, and begged for an audition, promising them that I really did speak English.

I could have sworn that they took the tape and canned it 'cause I didn't hear from them for months. Maybe six or seven months later, I got a phone call from somebody else saying that they were casting for a Spanish MTV show. I started doing MTV in Spanish and shortly after auditioned for MTV U.S.

ADAM CURRY I love Daisy. We always say that we were fortunate enough to sleep with each other just once. OK, it was on the red-eye from L.A. to New York. At least we slept together.

KEVIN SEAL I don't know how many harassing phone calls I gave Daisy, trying to get her interested in a Spanish language version of *The Avengers*. 'Cause I once saw Daisy in a catsuit and that was pretty much it for me for months. She would be a great Emma Peele.

STEVE LEEDS As we all know now, Daisy went on to be a Revlon model spokesperson. She's on commercial broadcast television now. Daisy evolved into a big worldwide celebrity. But when she came here, she had no skills other than that she was just naturally good at it.

House of Style

SHOW HOSTS Cindy Crawford, Daisy Fuentes, Rebecca Romijn-Stamos, Shalom Harlow, and Amber Valetta

CINDY CRAWFORD *House of Style* started out strictly fashion, but it evolved over the years. It was primarily for women, but knowing that MTV has a lot of male viewers, I'm sure that's why we did a lot of swimsuit editions and things like that. And it became a place where music and fashion met, so I think we had a lot of male viewers for that reason, too.

I never really felt like it was my show. I really felt like I was part of a *House of Style* team, which for me was even more fun because it was one of the first times in my work experience where I was part of the team. As a model you show up at the job, they hand you the dress you're going to wear, and they tell you smile or don't smile, and it's not much give and take. And with *House of Style*, I would sometimes go to preproduction meetings where we would talk about ideas, or if I was doing an exciting shoot, I would say, "Hey, do you guys want to cover this shoot? Or do you want to come with me to my tenth-year high school reunion?" Obviously, that made me feel like part of it, just being able to share my ideas, some of which definitely got the thumbs-down. But once in a while I had a good idea and it would be a place for me to just be part of that creative process.

And yes, *House of Style* did actually go to my tenth reunion. Although they *did* leave before I started singing the girl's part of "Paradise by the Dashboard Light."

ALISON STEWART It was so much fun to be a segment producer on *House of Style* because we do some serious, serious makeup. You could just go, "Oh, I'm going to play with hair toys now." I went to Hawaii, went to the bottom of a volcano, learned to make surfboards. It was weird, too. Cindy Crawford is a really big star, and I have to admit I was a little starstruck. I came in and found her on my phone once, and I was just like, "Oh, *Cindy Crawford's* on my phone."

CINDY CRAWFORD At one of the Video Music Awards, I was interviewing Chris Robinson from the Black Crowes and he had these really cool suede pants on with some embroidery up the legs. I said, "Those are really cool pants, Chris. Where'd you get 'em?"

He said, "My stylist got them for me. They have cannabis leaves down the side." Without even thinking, I said, "What's cannabis?"

Cindy Crawford

1989–95

CINDY CRAWFORD I was twenty-one or twenty-two when I got the call from MTV. At that time, my modeling career was taking off. I'd been on a few covers. I'd just done *Playboy*, which was a big deal.

I don't even think I was nervous. I didn't know enough to be nervous. Two years later I saw the show and I was like, "Oh my God, how embarrassing."

DAVE SIRULNICK, news and production executive You'd never have so many friends as the times when you'd have a meeting with Cindy in your office. Every guy you ever said "hi" to anywhere in this building would have to come by and say, "Hey Dave, did you see the game? Oh, sorry, am I interrupting? Oh, hi, Cindy, hi." You know, she'd be sitting there for an hour and you'd have fourteen people come by.

CINDY CRAWFORD Being affiliated with MTV, everyone thinks that you know what the cool music is, that you have a hip factor. I did know about fashion, but when it came to music and bands I was pretty clueless. My producer, Alisa Bellettini, would always say, "Listen, if someone interviews you and they ask you who your favorite band is, if you say Bonnie Raitt, I'm gonna kill you."

KURT LODER Cindy is a very smart woman. She's beautiful and smart. *House of Style* used to ask me to write for Cindy. We shot something in my office one day. Cindy came in, I was dressed as I usually am. She said, "Who dressed you this morning? Your mother?" She, of course, looked fabulous. I just looked like a shlump.

CINDY CRAWFORD I got to interview Will Smith, before he was the huge megastar that he is today. We went on the set of *Fresh Prince of Bel Air*. They tried to dress me kind of street, hip-hop. Somehow I ended up with a pair of Air Jordans and they were new. I had seen a thing where some rap guy was talking about how it's cool to leave the tag on. So I'm interviewing Will and we're shooting hoops. He said "Cool sneakers," and then he sees the tag and he says, "You're hip, you're in the know." I said, "Yeah, Humpty Dumpty told me to do that." And I remember Will's face. He was like, "It's Humpty, not Humpty Dumpty."

ROBERT LAFORTY, production executive On my thirtieth birthday, we were all having dinner. Cindy had these big Coke cans in her hair to keep it really curly. She sang "Happy Birthday" to me at a table full of people. How many guys could say, on their thirtieth birthday Cindy Crawford—in curlers—sang "Happy Birthday" to them?

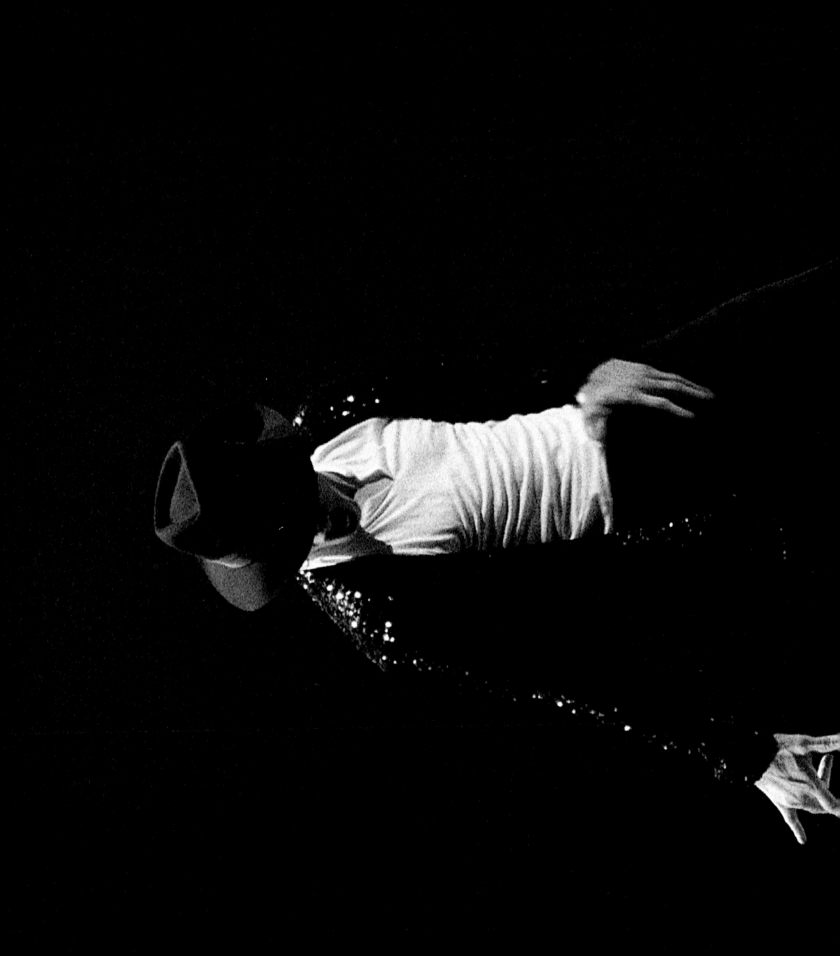

Michael Jackson

ICE CUBE I didn't watch MTV a lot, because they played a whole lot of corny kinds of video that I wasn't into. I didn't really start watching until they played Michael Jackson. When they started playing Michael Jackson, that's when they got a fan out of me.

TOM FRESTON, MTV chairman and CEO Michael Jackson injected MTV with a huge sense of possibility, that major new types of artists—who have a whole song-and-dance routine, essentially, with clever video editing, and big budgets—could really shape this medium.

KURT LODER Michael Jackson sent around a release at one point where all the VJs were told they had to refer to him as the King of Pop. This was just really offensive. And they didn't even approach us about that in the news department.

DAVE SIRULNICK We could not get over the fact that they had the audacity to actually do this, that he was sort of crowning himself, and we just thought this was the craziest thing in the world. And they were serious about it, Michael was serious about a lot of these kinds of things at that time. He liked awards, and he liked being honored, and he really thought he was the King of Pop and wanted to be referred to that way. Well, you know, of course, as soon as we got that, and put it in Kurt Loder's hands, for the next decade, it was "the self-proclaimed King of Pop."

ADAM CURRY We wanted to give Michael Jackson the Video Vanguard Award. And he said, "I want Adam Curry to come and give this to me." I went out with Tom Freston. We did a little ceremony. It was really trippy walking into MJJ Studios. There's like fifteen kids running around, a really weird scene.

So we're setting up and Michael was wearing these shiny vinyl pants. There's one guy whose only job was to Windex him and keep him shiny the whole time. And Michael is not a small guy. I'm six-foot-three or six-foot-four and he's probably about six-foot-one. So we're getting ready to do the award and the camera is getting set up and he leans and there's a little whispering going on and someone runs off and comes back with a box because he had to look taller than I was. So he's standing on an apple crate like seven feet tall. Just totally bizarre.

SISQO Michael Jackson in 1995 was the music performer of the decade. He performed for about fifteen minutes. He came back and solidified that he was still *the man*. He just came out there and captivated the world the same way as when he came out and moon-walked across the stage on Motown 25. We were all watching.

VMA 1995

DATE September 7
LOCATION Radio City Music Hall, New York
HOST Dennis Miller

PERFORMERS

Bon Jovi	"Something for the Pain"/ "Helter Skelter"
Green Day	"Basketcase"
Hole	"Doll Parts"
Hootie and the Blowfish	"Only Wanna Be with You"
Michael Jackson	"Don't Stop Till You Get Enough"/"The Way You Make Me Feel"/"Black or White"/"Thriller"/"Beat It"/ "Dirty Diana"/"Smooth Criminal"/"Billie Jean"/ "Dangerous"/"Theme from The Good, The Bad, and The Ugly"/"You Are Not Alone"/"The Way You Make Me Feel"
Live	"I Alone"
Alanis Morissette	"You Oughtta Know"
Red Hot Chili Peppers	"Warped"
R.E.M.	"Wake Up Bomb"
TLC	"Creep"/"Ain't 2 Proud 2 Beg"/"Waterfalls"
White Zombie	"More Human Than Human"

WINNERS

Best Video	TLC, "Waterfalls"
Best Male Video	Tom Petty and the Heartbreakers, "You Don't Know How It Feels"
Best Female Video	Madonna, "Take a Bow"
Best Group Video	TLC, "Waterfalls"
Best Rap Video	Dr. Dre, "Keep Their Heads Ringin'"
Best Dance Video	Michael and Janet Jackson, "Scream"
Best Metal/ Hard Rock Video	White Zombie, "More Human Than Human"
Best Alternative Music Video	Weezer, "Buddy Holly"
Best New Artist	Hootie and the Blowfish, "Hold My Hand"
Breakthrough Video	Weezer, "Buddy Holly"
Video Vanguard	R.E.M.
Viewer's Choice	TLC, "Waterfalls"

TABITHA SOREN Madonna was very difficult to get to sit down and interview at a big awards show. She's finally with Kurt, and we were all trying to get this interview done quickly. All of a sudden, these compacts, makeup, is being thrown through the middle of the shot. I thought it's just some fan, and that's really obnoxious.

KURT LODER Things started whizzing past our heads. Then we heard this drunken shrieking down on the ground, 'cause it was on an elevated stage. We looked down and it was Courtney Love, and she was throwing compacts, throwing whatever was around, staggering around, just out of her mind.

TABITHA SOREN She had lipstick smeared all over her face, hanging out of her dress, and she was not looking her best.

KURT LODER And Maddie's going, "Please, don't invite her up here. I think she wants attention."

TABITHA SOREN ...as if those two women don't get enough attention.

KURT LODER But somebody in my earpiece was saying, "Get her up! It'll be great! They'll be Jell-O wrestling or something..."

TABITHA SOREN I remember thinking *Courtney is not gonna like this tomorrow morning when she sees it on TV.* And Madonna was totally trying to be very graceful. But her publicist was going, "Cut! Cut! Cut! Get her out of there. Get Madonna out of there! I don't even want her in the same shot as this train wreck."

ALISON STEWART, news producer I remember standing at the bottom of the stairs watching that whole thing happen. Courtney Love's manager was at the bottom of the stairs saying, "They'll never use this, they'll never use this." And we were like, "It's live, doofus, it's on!"

KURT LODER Madonna finally made her retreat, totally dignified, really looking like the voice of reason. Courtney remained. At one point, I think at the end, she was sitting on a stool, and she was so out of it, she just toppled off the stool, with her legs wide apart, facing the camera crew, who all, in unison, turned away and looked at each other. She had bruises all over her thighs, not a pretty sight.

TABITHA SOREN The clash of the divas. And Kurt was in the middle of it, loving every minute.

Bill Bellamy

1992–98

BILL BELLAMY I got started on the channel on a beautiful day in '92. I was at the Boston comedy club in New York City and a lady came up to me after a set and said, "Hi, I work for MTV and I'm looking for a host for this new show called *MTV Jams*." I couldn't believe it. I thought she was just joking around 'cause New York is always scamming, "Hey bro, you want some sunglasses? You want some sunblockers?" It's always something. To make a long story short, I came in for an audition and I got the job. I had no idea I would ever be a VJ.

The first big interview I remember having was Janet Jackson. That was pretty intense. I was very much a fan first before I interviewed her, so I was sort of intoxicated at the time and I came to the set and I was like ur ur ur ur ur ur ur ur. And everybody's saying, "Bill, relax, it's just Janet Jackson." I'm thinking; Oh lord, oh lord, its Janet Jackson, that's Penny from *Good Times*, that's Michael Jackson's sister, that's Latoya's niece. I was going crazy, you know? So I was like, "Oh my God, how can I interview this woman?" "That's the Way Love Goes" was her big song and she was feeling all over me.

KENNEDY That's what all the women always did with Bill. There is one thing you could count on, any woman that he interviewed, some of the most famous women in the world, were just reduced to flirtatious fourteen-year-olds.

karen duffy
1991–93

Kennedy

1992–94

PAULY SHORE Kennedy had a crush on me. She told me so. She used to work at K-Rock, out here in Los Angeles, the radio station. And I used to go in there and do interviews and she liked me a lot. I wanted to have sex with Kennedy, but yeah, she always thought that I didn't like her because she wasn't a bimbo. You know what I mean. She didn't have the big fake boobs and the blond hair and talk like th-is.

JOHN NORRIS Kennedy's great. Her VJ tenure and my VJ/news tenure kind of overlapped so we ended up working together a lot and had this cool kind of vibe. We had this cool kind of brother-sister thing; you know, we had a good time together, but we also would bicker a lot. We would definitely disagree. When we got into the political arena we were definitely on opposite sides of the spectrum. A lot of those conversations were off-camera.

KENNEDY I was an intern on the morning show at K-Rock and I was also a part-time DJ on the overnights. A woman from MTV called the producer of the morning show and she said they needed people. She asked, "How about Kennedy?" and the producer said, "You mean the intern on the morning show?" So I went and I met with her and I had like four interviews. They said, "We're about to change our lineup. How would you like to come to New York?" I loved New York. I had been there in high school so I signed up right away. I flew out to New York on a Saturday night and I was on MTV Monday morning.

It was the most nerve-racking thing that I could have ever imagined. I thought there would be a couple of weeks of rehearsals and lighting and measuring and prep and "how you doing" and cocktail parties. But nope, Duff was on vacation, had to fill her slot. So I was like the stiff girl.

Nirvana
Unplugged

BETH MCCARTHY MILLER, director I was very nervous—you know, this is about five months before Kurt Cobain ended up killing himself. We shot that in November and he died in April. So everyone was just nervous and making sure everybody was happy and that Nirvana was happy and that this was gonna happen. And so Kurt comes out and we start rehearsing. There's a little downtime and I'm talking to the lighting designer and a couple of people in the control room. Then I turn around and my camera guy is up by Kurt Cobain talking. He was basically asking him if he could move the microphone a little bit on his close-up vocal. It looked better, but I had no idea what he was talking to him about. It was like, "Oh my God! What is he doing? Get him away from him!" But he was so nice and sweet. Kurt came to the control room after the show and he watched a couple of songs and said, "It looks really great. The only request is there's a couple of times after the songs that I smile. Can you make sure you go to a spot of me smiling? 'Cause I'm trying to show a different side of myself."

ALEX COLETTI, executive producer This whole thing was plotted out very carefully.

THERESA BEYERS Every song that they chose to perform was a poem to Kurt Cobain.

ALEX COLETTI He was the one who suggested the stargazer lilies, those big white lilies and he wanted more candles like a funeral. He said, "Yeah, yeah, like a funeral. That'll be cool."

JUDY MCGRATH Musically, one of the most unforgettable nights of my life. And in retrospect, truly unusual moments. Kurt signing autographs for a friend's young daughters, saying, "Please save them." Kurt taking me aside to tell me that one or two people in the Music Group Department "are very good employees, please take care of them." And then there was the set, the candles, the lighting. I still can't listen to "In the Pines" without feeling bereft.

Working at MTV: The 1990s

BRIAN GRADEN, president, programming and production They had a diversity pamphlet, championing the idea that all different kinds of people matter. There are more people of color, there are more gay people, there are more other points of view on MTV than anywhere else on television. And Tom Freston, who's the boss, also believes strongly in making sure the culture celebrates diversity. To me, that's the promise of music, at its best. We don't do well all the time, but this organization tries to make room for all people. I mean, I'm a gay guy and I'm running all the programming—atypical.

TED DEMME, producer We wore that MTV proudly. You'd walk down the halls and everyone's got a different MTV logo on: It's a hat, it's a *Yo* shirt, it's a *Club MTV* shirt, it's a *Remote Control* shirt, it's a new thing. I was going through my wardrobe before I got married so I could have room for my wife's stuff. Everything was an MTV shirt. It was like we were in this weird fraternity.

DAN CORTESE I was making three hundred dollars a week as an office PA. Then when I got the *MTV Sports* job it just kicked my income up to four hundred dollars a week.

CINDY CRAWFORD It was the first time that I got to feel like part of the real working world. I would go to the *HOS* offices and be part of production meetings, and meet with Alisa about different ideas that we could do in the future. And I think that gave another dimension to my whole working life. It made me sometimes appreciate going back to straight modeling where I didn't have to have ideas.

GEORGE EPLEY, technical operations executive One of the jokes among the production engineers is that you are always nice to the person who's going to hand you the script, because they are going to be the producer of the next show you work on.

ADAM CURRY If anyone thinks you make big dough at MTV you are wrong. It was good money, I'm not going to knock it. But that was basically spent upgrading myself to first class and paying for limos so I wouldn't look like a schmuck when I arrived somewhere. So, I really was left with nothing, and what money I had, a couple hundred grand, I put into my company and that has successfully turned around to give me a good return on the investment.

KEVIN SEAL My job at MTV, what my actual work day was like—the day before, I would get a little schedule faxed to me about what time I was supposed to be there. I put it in the wastebasket. Otherwise it filled the place up with trash. The next day, it was two or three o'clock, the telephone rings for the fourth or fifth time, and I agree to go to the studio. Play a little bit of Asteroids maybe. I finally decide it's time to shower and then it's right to the craft service table. Those were good days. There

were some days where it couldn't be put off anymore and you had to go tape something. Then you go sit down on some part of the set, the couch that's made of the back end of an old Chevy. The crazy-looking bar that looks like it's in a diner but really isn't.

ROBERT LAFORTY, former executive I love getting in the elevators 'cause you never know what you're going to see—an executive in a suit standing next to an intern, or a PA in shorts with a nose ring, three earrings, and purple hair.

DAVE SIRULNICK You know, other places have sort of dress-down Fridays. This is like a dress-down decade. You could look up, you know, and two people are having a light saber fight down the hall and someone else is skateboarding by.

MARK DOCTROW, producer I pitched an idea to cover Madonna recording her new album. Months later my boss pops his head into my office and says, "Madonna said yes, we're going to L.A. on Thursday." We get to the studio and they are in the middle of recording. Here I am trying to concentrate on shooting and producing but at the same time I'm, you know, wanting to listen to the music. It turns out that she's laying down vocals for one of the songs, called "Skin," and she's actually going to let us shoot it. And like anyone, she kinda doesn't want everyone on top of her while she's singing. Madonna quickly looks around the room and assesses the situation and just says, "Everybody that doesn't have to be here, get out." I had a little camera, so she says, "You can stay." At that point I am not realizing what that means. I'm just panicking 'cause I want to make sure I've got the right tape in. All of a sudden I look around and realize that I'm alone in the recording booth with Madonna. It was just one of those moments where you're just sort of like, "How did I get here?"

DAVE SIRULNICK We had an intern one time, you'd leave every night, you'd be leaving at nine, nine-thirty, ten o'clock, and this one guy would always be in this

one room sort of watching tapes or dubbing something, working hard. You'd come back the next morning, sometimes really early, and he'd still sort of be there and you'd start talking. "Did you know that, did you see that guy?" Well it turned out for about five weeks, this kid lived here. He just lived in this little cubicle for about five weeks because he had nowhere else to go and he wanted to stay at MTV and didn't want to pay rent and he would just stay there, stay here all the time. Interns are always a source of great interest and amusement around the halls of MTV.

DAVE SIRULNICK Hammer is coming by to deliver one of his big production videos. He's got his entourage of people with him. He marches up to the elevators and this security guard steps in front of Hammer. "What's your business, sir?" Hammer just sort of looks at him. "Don't you know who I am?" "No." "Well I'm going upstairs." "No you're not!" And the guy doesn't let Hammer come up.

CHRIS KRESKI, writer It was the VMAs at the Universal Amphitheater and Sting was on the show. It was the year the bee girl finished the show. The show's over and the audience is going out the back. I'm standing right at the wing of the stage and the celebrities are funneling forward, up the stage and out toward the press tent. I'm standing in the corner

looking out toward them and the person I'm talking to is looking at me. I do a double-take and I see Sting halfway through the audience and I don't know him, I've never met him, yet he's looking at me like he's happy to see me.

He's kind of waving. I kind of give a little half-wave back. I didn't know what to do. And he's coming up toward the stage to head out and trying to make eye contact and I'm completely flustered. He finally comes up and says, "Oh my God, I haven't seen you in so long," and he hugs me. This big bear hug, and I'm like doing the little pat on the back. I didn't know what to do. I'm like, "Great to see you." He's like, "Whatever you do, I'll be at the press tent, find me." No idea who I was.

Some of the mean people said he thought I was probably Phil Collins.

ANDREA DUNCAN, news writer/producer There's a lot of rappers that are into feet. I was doing an interview with DMX. When we started the interview, he was like, "Oh, you have got great feet." He kept looking at them during the interview and at one point he stopped the interview to comment on them again. Later that day my coproducer was trying to get a shot

of Redman walking down the street. And he was really not cooperating. He kept talking to me about my feet and where I got them done, and could he get me an anklet. He was asking why I didn't wear an anklet, 'cause my feet would be so much cuter with an anklet. From then on I just decided if I ever do interviews during the summer I'm going to wear sandals, and I'm going to get my toes done because it seems to really help the interview. It kind of breaks the ice a little bit.

ROGER COLETTI, MTV radio producer Over the years I have done hundreds of interviews for MTV. Ozzy Osbourne is one of my favorite people to talk to. Aside from being very funny, he's also one of the nicest guys I have ever met. I think it was in April 2000, I interviewed the Oz for the 2000 Ozzfest tour. The interview took place a week before one of my best friends' wedding. Joe is a big Ozzy fan so I thought it would be nice to have Ozzy sign my invitation as part of a wedding gift. Anyway, Ozzy was happy to do it and wrote, "To Joe and Tina . . . Have Lots of Sex! Ozzy Osbourne." At first Joe did not believe it was real—but then I showed him the photo of me and Ozzy. The invitation is now hanging up in his house. Thanks, Ozzy.

MTV's an interesting place to work. Especially if, like myself (briefly, long ago), you ever worked at a small-town newspaper and found yourself nodding through, say, a local town-council meeting. Working at MTV is more interesting than that in every way. It's also interesting in a different way just about every day.

Given the nature of news—and of the show-biz precincts that we generally patrol at MTV News—it is perhaps not surprising that we should be confronted practically every morning with fresh instances of startling, shocking, or head-slappingly stupid behavior. Can Prince really have decided to change his name to an unpronounceable symbol? Can a sharp and mega-successful businessman like Puffy Combs really have gotten himself mixed up in a tawdry nightclub shoot-out? Can Michael Jackson's minions really believe that by simply faxing out an order that all future news stories about the star refer to him as "the King of Pop," we'll be cowed into doing so? (This actually happened; the News Department ignored the decree.)

Then there's the river of celebrities that sploshes through MTV's New York studios every week. You haven't lived until you've witnessed the talented but curiously sourpussed rapper-turned-movie-star Mark Wahlberg attempting to snub Eminem during a *TRL* taping, and heard Eminem vaporize him with an impromptu jibe about Wahlberg's not-all-that-long-ago Funky Bunch past. Or watched a puzzled audio tech wondering where, exactly, to attach a lavaliere microphone to a barely clothed Lil' Kim. (Clip it on a nipple? Nail it to her head?) Or flattened yourself against a hallway wall in order to allow pop princess Britney Spears to pass by with her enveloping cloud of handlers, flacks, and security bruisers, in a formation reminiscent of a holiday parade float.

As with so many things in life, the presence of celebrity eventually loses its novelty. One can become jaded.

Fortunately, at MTV there's an unending influx of new, young employees, whose enthusiasm is a tonic to those of us who've been there for...well, forever, practically. Since the company promotes from within, it's entirely possible for someone to start out as a lowly production assistant during a school break, then return after graduation and, within a few years, work his or her way up to the rank of full-fledged producer. In pursuit of this possibility, young MTV News staffers work ridiculous hours tracking down stories by day, logging tapes late into the night, and—in those rare hours when they're not living their lives entirely at the office—trolling obscure clubs in search of new acts and new sounds. That they are able to do all this on a diet composed almost entirely of lukewarm bottled water and hastily gulped handfuls of vending-machine candy is some kind of awesome tribute to our national genetic fiber, I think. And surely they must be motivated by more than the promise of a fleeting glimpse of Christina Aguilera as she jibbers her way down some studio corridor.

My own interactions with the ambient celebrities at 1515 Broadway these days are fairly low-key. A few years ago, though, I was sitting in the studio makeup room when a thin young blonde woman in the chair next to me—whose presence I'd barely registered—got up and left, and somebody said, "That was Heather Graham." My most enduring memory of Graham was in her role as the hapless teenage runaway in *Drugstore Cowboy* ten years earlier. Feeling I'd breached some unspoken celebrity protocol, I made my way to the Green Room, where the actress was waiting to go on-set, and apologized for not having acknowledged her presence. I'm a big fan, I said; loved you in *Drugstore Cowboy*, but you look so (duh) different now...and so forth and so on. Heather Graham looked at me, clearly perplexed, and said, "Do I know you?"

—KURT LODER

Jenny McCarthy

1995–97

GILBERT GOTTFRIED I remember being on Jenny McCarthy, well—on her show. I'd like to be on Jenny McCarthy, but I was just on her show. What she would do to greet me was, she would run forward, scream out, leap up in the air, wrap her legs around my waist and her arms around my neck, and I'd support her weight by putting my hands under her butt. We did this a few takes because I'm a professional. And we wanted to make sure we had just the right shot. So I would have her keep running forward, jumping, wrapping her legs around me and me holding onto her butt, just because I care. I care that it looks professional. I'm from the old school of show business. I want things to work well.

JENNY McCARTHY I went to my manager's office and on his desk there was a fax that said, "MTV auditions for a female host for a dating game show." I thought, *I have to do this.* I told my manager to get on this. He called MTV and said, "You have to see this girl," and they said, "Absolutely not, we don't want anything to do with a *Playboy* Playmate." He must have called at least ten more times that day. Finally they said, "Bring her in."

There must have been three or four hundred girls in line all standing there. I remember thinking, *Oh man, what the hell am I gonna do?* I went in the little room, did a little improv, and they asked me for my head shot and I didn't have one yet. So I drew a picture on a piece of paper with my phone number on it and I got a call back.

JOE DAVOLA There was sort of a negative contingent from the women at MTV for Jenny McCarthy because of her *Playboy* background. We had *Singled Out.* I was looking at her audition tape and saying this girl is great. She has something. But it's gonna be a major hurdle to get her on the air. People started rolling their eyes when they saw her, but she really became a good comedian. That won the women over.

JENNY McCARTHY When I first got the show, I knew I had three minutes of camera time each show, and that's nothing. So every time I saw that red light go on on the camera, I made sure people knew who I was. That was my mission. So when I got the phone call from *Rolling Stone* I went, "All right, mission accomplished." The girl with the most mustard— that's the way they put it.

Singled Out

PREMIERE June 5, 1995

JENNY MCCARTHY The first *Singled Out* was *Spring Break* at Lake Havasu and it was a nightmare. The night before, I was in my hotel room and my boyfriend at the time was really sick. He was up all night. I couldn't stay up with him so I lit a little candle for him in the bathroom and I put it on top of my hot rollers and I went to sleep. Well, something in my dream that night was saying to wake up, because I was so out. I just opened up my eyes a little bit and the room was filled with black smoke. There were flames coming out of the bathroom. I mean, full-blown, ready-to-die fire. I started screaming and my boyfriend grabbed me and ran me out of the room and the fire department came. There must have been twenty firemen putting it out. Our faces were black and we were coughing up black chunks and the fireman told us five more minutes and we would have been dead. It literally burned the ceiling to the next floor. and The room was just trashed in black smoke. I had to be on the set in two hours. So I sneezed and coughed up black goo and got onstage and that was the first show. You can't tell though—I gave it my all.

The MTV people were freaking out for me. I thought they were gonna say, "You idiot! What did you do? We're gonna get another girl." But they said, "We'll cancel the show right now. We won't shoot today. Are you sure you're OK?" They made sure my safety was first, which is odd out here. But they were really concerned. I said no, let's do it. I've been dying to do it, let's do it. Because it took a year from the time I got the first show, so I was anxiously awaiting this moment and then I light a room on fire.

I was excited and also feeling a little ill because I had full carbon monoxide poisoning. It was so bad, but I remember the adrenaline got me through the show. The last thing I remember was me and Chris looked at the camera and said, "See you this summer!" I thought, *Yeah, we did it!* I did it and I am alive.

The first season was tough because no one knew who I was. I wasn't anybody. I was just this blond chick in a miniskirt and go-go boots. The guys basically treated me like crap. I was their bartender bitch basically. I had to stand up onstage with fifty guys and they were so rude. They would say, "I've seen better legs on a table." and they would grab and squeeze me and pull my hair. It was literally like being molested. It got to the point where I said to myself, "Just wait till the cameras roll, buddy, because that's when I take control and that's why I basically beat the crap out of the guys." The ones I really made fun of were the ones that were making fun of me before the show. By the time the second season began, people saw the show and the guys were a little bit more timid. They just kind of stared and I liked it that way. Stay away.

I had fun with it, making fun of the boys, beating them up and then rooting for the girls. 'Cause I was on their side. It was really funny to see how nervous they were. I mean, just 5-year-old little boys, just shaking up there. What control. I miss that.

Rock 'n' Jock

On April 1, 1990, MTV premiered its first sporting event with *MTV's Rock 'N Jock Diamond Derby*, featuring major-league baseball players and some of the hottest stars of rock 'n' roll and television. *Rock 'N Jock* raised money for the T. J. Martell Foundation for leukemia, cancer, and AIDS research.

20 Questions for 20 Years

DAVID SILVERIA—KORN

What song best describes your current state of mind? ———

What is your favorite video of all time? — "Learning to Fly," Foo Fighters

What is your first memory of MTV? — Martha Quinn and the OG song with the Moon Man.

Where were you the first time you saw yourself on MTV and how did you react? — The first time I saw myself on MTV I felt like crying.

Does the video enhance or hinder the song? — A video can help or fuck up a song. Good director—help/Bad director—fuck up

What is the most memorable moment you've witnessed on MTV? — I'll never forget winning "Best Rock Video" in 1999. We finally got to say "Here we are, if you don't like us—fuck off!"

Whose video work do you most admire? — I most admire McG for his video work. I've watched him come up through the years and now he's making movies.

What do you like most about MTV? — ———

What do you like least about MTV? — There are a few dumb shows on MTV

What is your favorite guilty pleasure video? — ———

What do you consider to be MTV's greatest achievement and/or greatest failure in its first twenty years? — MTV has done a great job keeping up with the times. We could have done without some of the shows, but it's all good. Hats off to you MTV!

What is the worst reaction you've received to one of your videos? — ———

Videos should . . . — ———

The best band name — ———

The greatest moment in rock and pop and rap was . . . — The greatest moment in pop has got to be the Backstreet Boys. Greatest moment in rock—Korn. Greatest moment in rap—Dr. Dre.

My biggest influence — ———

My favorite VMA performance — My favorite VMA performance has to be Blink-182. I love how they do their thing and don't give a fuck, but they are still good.

If I were president of MTV I would . . . — ———

What artist would you most like to work with and what would you like to do with them? — ———

Did video kill the radio star? — I don't care if video killed the radio star 'cause video is more fun. But I remember that was the first video played on MTV soooo, fuck it.

ROBERT SMALL, co-creator We wanted people to do things they hadn't done before. Which is why Aerosmith sitting down to do it was a cool thing and Eric Clapton redesigned his music—that was special.

JOEL GALLEN, producer The turning point of *Unplugged* was when Joe Walsh sat at a piano and sang "Desperado." In order to have that air we needed permission from Don Henley. We called him, we wrote him letters. Finally, we got a letter back from Don Henley two pages long saying how protective of this song he is. And he didn't want it to be done in the wrong atmosphere. Our talent person at the time, Abby Konowitch, called him up and said "OK, then why don't you come on and do *Unplugged*? Show us how it's really done." And so Don Henley was our first marquee star.

ALEX COLETTI, executive producer It was the first time we had an artist who could carry a whole show. Don brought background vocalists, he brought string players. The level of musicians that he had, the quality of players, the thought he put into the arrangements, was unprecedented at that time. Before it was more of a hootenanny jam, let's-figure-it-out-in-the-dressing-room kind of approach. And now here was a show that was rehearsed.

Don Henley allowed us to pursue Paul McCartney and Eric Clapton. Now all of a sudden people knew about *Unplugged* and wanted to do it. And they saw this as a vehicle.

Squeeze/Syd Straw/Jules Shear	11/26/89
Smithereens/Graham Parker	1/29/90
10,000 Maniacs/Michael Penn	2/5/90
The Alarm/Nuclear Valdez	2/11/90
Joe Walsh/Dr. John	2/18/90
Michelle Shocked/Indigo Girls	3/11/90
Sinéad O'Connor/The Church	3/18/90
Stevie Ray Vaughan/Joe Satriani	3/4/90
Don Henley	4/22/90
Damn Yankees/Great White	5/6/90
Crowded House/Tim Finn	5/13/90
Hall and Oates	6/5/90
Elton John	8/5/90
Crosby, Stills and Nash	9/30/90

VAN TOFFLER Dylan's managers couldn't find him for a week leading up to his *Unplugged*. He showed up a couple days before; he sometimes goes underground and disappears.

JOEL GALLEN Paul McCartney wanted to do it in England. So I flew over there, initially just to have a meeting with Paul and Linda. We set an approximate date when to do it. At the time *Unplugged* was only a half-hour show. I said we'd really like you to do an hour. 'Cause you're Paul McCartney, you have a lot of songs to do. He said, "No, I think a half-hour's plenty. Leave the audience wanting more." I said, "How can we come all the way over to England. It would cost us so much money, we only get five, six Paul McCartney songs? That's crazy." He said he was into doing a lot of the old songs he hadn't done in a long time. He wasn't going to play anything new. It was just so refreshing to see somebody who wanted to do it just for the sake of doing it.

We made all the arrangements, we're ready to go and it's now mid to late January and a little thing called Operation: Desert Storm hits. Everywhere there were threats of terrorism and bombs on planes. It just wasn't safe. They had tanks at Heathrow airport.

So we called McCartney's people to reschedule this thing, and they said, "Hey, look, Paul's a very busy guy. If we want to do a Paul McCartney *Unplugged* this is the week he's available." I had to go to all the powers, and I said, "I'll sign a waiver, I'll do whatever." Maybe there was a risk, in hindsight, but I felt Paul McCartney's an artist that I always wanted to work with and I felt it was important that I do it. Maybe it was the fan in me talking.

They wouldn't let anybody else go from MTV, my usual team that I would bring with me to these shows. I flew over there and put together a different team through MTV Europe. I get there, it's a few days before the show and Paul invites me to his home, two hours north of London, in some farm community. He has this barn that he's converted into a recording/rehearsal space. It's very small. And he said, "Let me run this set for you, tell me what you think." So I'm sitting on a couch, and his whole band is right in front of me. And he's doing the show just for me. I'm thinking, remember he was going to do a half-hour show, like five or six songs? So I'm thinking that's going to be it, right? He rolls off like twenty-two, twenty-three songs. It just never stops. As he got into rehearsing with the band, he said, "What about this song? What about this song?" They just loved it so much. So it was all happening through such a beautiful, natural process.

As he was doing some of the old Beatles songs, he's reading all the lyrics off a lyric sheet. I know all the words to the Beatles songs, and I didn't write them. How does he not know the words to "We Can Work It Out" or "And I Love Her"? I asked him afterward. He said he hadn't performed a lot of these songs since he recorded them twenty-five, twenty-eight years previously. In all that time, he probably had never even picked up a guitar and played any of them. He had written so many songs since then, he had to relearn them.

JOE PEROTA, director Once Michael Stipe pulled me
aside. We did some rehearsal, and then there was a
break and the band was going to leave and come
back later for the show. He said to me, "I really don't
want to leave my lyric book unattended. Do you think
you could watch that for me?" I'm the biggest R.E.M.
fan of all time. No problem. I took it and as soon as he
left, I ran back behind that set, I opened that book,
and I started looking at all these lyrics. And I had no
idea what they were. Nobody did. Alex Coletti came
with me. Michael Stipe's lyric book was just a lot of
shorthand that only he understood. I felt like I was
looking at James Bond's codebook or something.
Scraps of paper, a grocery list. A dozen eggs, carton
of milk, and then all of a sudden a song, written out. It
was quite an intimate look into how a great artist's
mind works.

ALEX COLETTI We were shooting Oasis at the Royal Festival Hall in London. We did about five days of rehearsals. Day one, we got there and the band showed up. Noel showed up first and then the band and Liam finally showed up. Thirteen songs, they ran through them twice. Liam was wearing a green shirt, green shorts, green Hush Puppies, very coordinated. They ran the show twice, but Liam only sang the first time 'cause he wanted to save his voice. Next day, Liam showed up a little later wearing the same clothes. A little scruffier. Sang only about eight of the songs to save his voice. Band runs through everything. Third day, Liam shows up very late. He's wearing the same clothes, he sings about five songs. Wanted to save his voice. Now we move the show to the Royal Festival Hall, day of the show. Liam shows up, wearing the same clothes. He sings one song and decides he can't go on, he's sick. Liam is rushed to a doctor. Doctor says he can't go on.

We've got the entire MTV crew, the record label, all flown over to London. This is the only time we decided that we were only going to do one show. There were no other bands. It wasn't like we were doing Oasis one day and George Michael the next. This was all about Oasis. At this point we've gone through all our security measures, we felt we spun all our wheels on that. At the same time, the band and Noel were working really hard. I felt like Noel wrote all these songs and he's got a great voice. Maybe this is the beginning of the new Oasis or Noel's solo career. Let's do the show. Whether or not we air it, let's tape it. And Noel put on a brilliant show.

Halfway through the show, I was on headsets and somebody said, "Hey, Alex, look up in the opera box." And I turn and look and there's Liam. There's Patsy Kensit [his fiancée at the time], Kate Moss, and a bottle of champagne. He's not looking too sick to me at this point. I'm like, "That son of a bitch." We got a camera up, I just wanted it on tape. There was a point in the show where the crowd caught on. The camera swung around and the crowd caught on. They thought that maybe he was going to come down and give us a song. I thought maybe this is all a setup for this big moment. It never happened, but he did toast the crowd, which was mighty nice of him.

VAN TOFFLER, president, MTV and MTV2 In the middle of "Unledded" I went to the bathroom and Robert Plant abused me from the stage, saying, "You know the guy who runs MTV is going to take a pee right now? He started to say bad things about me with the microphone on. Maybe because he scratched "Ramble On" from the set list before he went on and I said, "That is the best Zeppelin song." and he goes, "Well, I can't sing it tonight."

You get to live a dream, in a sense, to sit front and center to watch a band that you grew up idolizing and couldn't get within a gazillion yards of every time they toured. Little did I know I'd actually be having a disagreement with him about a set list.

Tom Green

BRIAN MCFAYDEN First time I had to do the news on *TRL*. I was a little nervous. "And Tom Green has cancer of—" I can't even say the words. Testicular cancer. *Tom Green has testicular cancer.* I was worried that I couldn't say it without laughing. I mean it's a serious issue. I'm thinking this is another one of Tom Green's stunts. So I go to all the news editors. "Is this for real? I don't want to go downstairs and embarrass myself on *TRL*." Especially coming out of something upbeat. What a weird transition. I honestly didn't believe it because of all the stunts that he's pulled. I thought, OK he's suckered one on *TRL*. He's pulled the wool over our eyes. Got you!

TOM GREEN "The Bum Bum Song" was kind of an improvised thing. We were trying to give the captain of the SS *Spring Break* a fish sandwich at four o'clock in the morning. The security guards came and tried to kick me out of the captain's area. And as we were getting kicked out, I started rubbing my bum on everything and singing "The Bum Bum Song." "My bum is on the rail, as I'm walking down the stairs, it was the only thing I could put my bum on."

And people really liked that. I noticed, when I watched the show, it struck a chord with the youth of America. They liked "The Bum Bum Song." People would come up to me on the street and say, "My bum is on the rail. My bum is on the rail." I thought, *Wow,*

this really could be something. So we went into a recording studio in Seattle. We wrote sort of an elaborate version of the song, which we're all quite proud of, especially since it became a number one song in America on *TRL* with Carson Daly. We actually had to retire it, 'cause I heard that the Backstreet Boys and 98 Degrees and Britney Spears were all pissed off. I don't know if it was true, but I heard that 98 Degrees *didn't* like "The Bum Bum Song." Not a lot of accolades from *NSYNC. I don't want *NSYNC to kick the crap out of me. There's five of them. Against one. And they're in shape. They dance, and I'm all out of shape.

We had this cool idea for doing an interview with U2. It was during the band's tech-addled "Zoo TV" tour in 1992. We caught up with them after a show in Philadelphia and appropriated four of the huge video screens they were using. We lined these up across the stage, and then sat the four members of the band down backstage—out of sight—and trained cameras on each of their faces. An image of each face was then projected onto one of the monitors onstage. I positioned myself on a platform way out in the middle of the stadium, microphone in hand. The idea was to show an interview being conducted with four gigantic video heads—very "Zoo TV," we thought.

Unfortunately, after several hours of dicking around with this very complex technical setup, we couldn't get the audio to work right. It was very late, and getting cold, too, when Bono finally muttered, "Did anybody check the batteries?" That was generally the problem, he and The Edge said, when U2 had sound glitches.

Smack of palms onto foreheads. Scramble of audio technicians. Various components were pulled apart. Inside one was an AA battery, and, yes, it was dead. Very "Zoo TV."

—KURT LODER

VMA 1997

DATE September 4
LOCATION Radio City Music Hall, New York
HOST Chris Rock

PERFORMERS

Beck	"The New Pollution"
Spice Girls	"Say You'll Be There"
Jamiroquai	"Virtual Insanity"
Marilyn Manson	"The Beautiful People"
U2	"Please"
Prodigy	"Breathe"
Lil' Kim featuring Left-Eye Lopes, Missy Elliot, and Angie Martinez	"Not Tonight"
Sting, Puff Daddy, and Faith Evans	"I'll Be Missing You"
Jakob Dylan and Bruce Springsteen	"One Headlight"

WINNERS

Best Video	Jamiroquai, "Virtual Insanity"
Best Male Video	Beck, "Devil's Haircut"
Best Female Video	Jewel, "You Were Meant for Me"
Best Group Video	No Doubt, "Don't Speak"
Best Rap Video	The Notorious B.I.G., "Hypnotize"
Best Dance Video	Spice Girls, "Wannabe"
Best Rock Video	Aerosmith, "Falling in Love (Is Hard on the Knees)"
Best Alternative Music Video	Sublime, "What I Got"
Best New Artist	Fiona Apple, "Sleep to Dream"
Breakthrough Video	Jamiroquai, "Virtual Insanity"
Viewer's Choice	Prodigy, "Breathe"
Video Vanguard	L.L. Cool J

ICE CUBE I'm not easily moved, you know what I mean, but it was power. I had wished something similar was done for Tupac. I just commended them for putting it together like that and making sure that Biggie had a proper legacy.

DA BRAT Everything went wrong with everybody's wardrobe. I had to wear this big Trojan headpiece that kept sliding off my head. I had this hard breastplate thing and it was so heavy that I could barely walk. I had to carry a sword, it was really ridiculous. None of our clothes were right. I think Kim was upset because her stylist didn't show up with her stuff until later. Missy was mad because her stuff was not fitting right, and Angie Martinez was mad 'cause her stuff was too plain. So everybody had huge issues. But when we got out there you really couldn't see it. Li'l Kim almost fell but y'all did not hear that from me. And I think she almost tripped over my little sword 'cause I had dropped my sword.

GWEN STEFANI I remember seeing his little chicken cutlet butt-cheeks hanging out.

DAVE GROHL I was sitting next to my mom when he showed his big white ass to the audience. It was great. Then they showed the reaction of all the rappers in the audience and they were horrified because he was up there acting like the Antichrist.

Total Request Live

BRIAN GRADEN, president, programming and production Times Square is probably the center of the universe. And you can see the world changing behind you on a daily basis and I think people have the sense that if you tune in to *TRL* you're going to know exactly what's going on in the world—what movie's coming out, what video's hot, what people are talking about, what the news and the politics of the day are. I think it's just become the touchstone for the audience.

CARSON DALY We started it off like *Wayne's World.* It was like three or four camera guys in here that I'm friendly with, and we just really had fun in the early days. It slowly started to grow and grow and grow, and then we got a little bit bigger guests, and it was just slow and steady, which I think was important.

The beautiful thing about *TRL* is, unlike a talk show, we're not beholden to who's on the couch for ratings. The show is the star and the energy of being live. Since the crowd was already outside, we would do some stuff to bring them in.

I wanted the studio audience because I thought when I come on it would be kind of cool to have somebody to talk to. So, if I said, like, "Did anybody see Britney on the *Rolling Stone* cover? My God, what was she wearing?" I felt like it would be easier if I could say it to some friends. So I asked for it. They did it and right when they did it I felt it was like kind of a mistake 'cause I got like really really self-conscious.

It was so weird standing on *TRL* and these kids would just like stare at me waiting for something to happen. There's five thousand kids outside the windows. There are days when I'm up there and I feel like the world is watching and, unless you have tremendous self-confidence, it's a little weird.

ROB DIXTER, associate producer Janet Jackson was on. We had a girl out in Times Square who literally was crying. She had tears. She asked Janet her question and Janet said, "Hey Carson, can I invite this girl up?" And this girl was just bawling. She came in, and she didn't stop crying. Finally, at the end of the show, we tell her to go ahead, talk to Janet. She asked her for a hug or something like that. And Janet came over and hugged this girl. And this girl was holding on for dear life. Still crying, even after she hugged Janet. The crying doesn't stop on *TRL*.

DEBORAH GIBSON I do wish that ten or twelve years ago there was something like that for me. Now artists really get to connect with the audience more than ever. I love that—live performances in the studio or on the street surrounded by fans.

LANCE BASS The first time we went to *TRL*, no one really knew what it was, so there were just ten people outside. Then they moved to 1515 Broadway and every time we would come it would just get bigger and now it's just insane. They have to close down the streets.

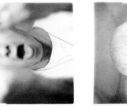

Carson Daly

1997–present

CARSON DALY I was twenty-two and had already worked at a bunch of radio stations. I just loved music. I loved having fun on the air and interviewing bands—most of them I was friends with. I was just kind of sitting there at KROQ. I had been there a year and I thought, "Well now what? What am I really going to do? Am I going to be a DJ the rest of my life?" And this opportunity came up to come to MTV to do what I did on radio, on television.

I was doing nights at KROQ, it was a very coveted position, six to ten at night in L.A. When I got the job a bit of a buzz was created in L.A. When new talent comes into that town, the agents in Hollywood just smell new blood.

GWEN STEFANI Carson is somebody we met years ago, when we just started out in '95. He was on a radio station up north. I remember we all came in with a six-pack of beer, it was like twelve noon, and we were like, "Hey, we're a rock group." We just hung out all afternoon. He was a cool guy. Next thing I know he's the MTV guy.

CARSON DALY I got a bunch of messages from agents and managers and people. *Details* did this big article on the "new kid." I was approached by MTV when they were doing their Beach House out in Motel California. They were looking for some part-time VJs just for the summer.

I did that for two-and-a-half months. At the end of the summer they asked me to move to New York.

I got off the plane and I just started drinking. I didn't know anything. I didn't know anybody in New York, even though I have family in Jersey. I came out with my mom. MTV put me up in this hotel. I just woke up every day and just came into this giant 1515 Broadway and was kind of like, "How's it going, everybody? I'm Carson Daly. I'm the new guy. We have a lot of work to do. Let's get this bad boy up and running."

Where I come from in radio, they don't have the luxury of seeing me and if I'm telling a good story about a girl whose bra came off in the mosh pit at the Rage show last night, I have to paint this visual picture. So I hated my first time live on MTV—I was nervous.

Because Los Angeles is such a sprawl, all of our *Week in Rock* trips out there involved long, long days of shooting. At the end of one of these, back in 1988, after about twelve hours of racing around town without even a lunch break, we finally wound up at the Hyatt House, the much-storied rock hotel on Sunset Boulevard, where we were scheduled to do an interview with the great Little Richard ("the king *and* queen of rock 'n' roll," as he was happy to be known), who actually lived there under his given name, Richard Penniman. We waited for him in the bar, where, to kill time, we (well, I) started knocking back neon-colored drinks of the kind that come with little paper umbrellas stuck in them. By the time Richard finally arrived, and started knocking back some himself . . . well, after a while, the cameraman wondered aloud if he should really keep shooting, what with all the hooting and hawing we were doing under the influence of these incapacitating cocktails. He was told to keep rolling, and the resulting footage, I believe, vividly demonstrates the benefits of liquor in livening up the average interview. (By the way, one of the great, unadvertised TV perks in situations like this is that someone other than yourself—generally a production-management person with a bagful of cash strapped to his waist—winds up paying the bill.)

—KURT LODER

VMA 1996

DATE September 4
LOCATION Radio City Music Hall, New York
HOST Dennis Miller

David Lee Roth reunites with members of Van Halen for the first time in ten years.

PERFORMERS

Smashing Pumpkins	"Tonight, Tonight"
Fugees	"Fu-Gee-La"/"Killing Me Softly"/"Ready or Not"
Fugees and Nas	"If I Ruled the World"
Metallica	"Until It Sleeps"
L.L. Cool J	"Doin' It"
Neil Young	"The Needle and the Damage Done"
Hootie and the Blowfish	"Sad Caper"
Alanis Morissette	"Your House"
Bush	"Machinehead"
The Cranberries	"Salvation"
Oasis	"Champagne Supernova"
Bone Thugs-N-Harmony	"Tha Crossroads"
KISS	"Rock and Roll All Night"

WINNERS

Best Video	Smashing Pumpkins "Tonight, Tonight"
Best Male Video	Beck, "Where It's At"
Best Female Video	Alanis Morissette, "Ironic"
Best Group Video	Foo Fighters, "Big Me"
Best Rap Video	Coolio featuring LV, "Gangsta's Paradise"
Best Dance Video	Coolio, "1,2,3,4 (Sumpin' New)"
Best Hard Rock Video	Metallica, "Until It Sleeps"
Best Alternative Music Video	Smashing Pumpkins, "1979"
Best R&B Video	Fugees (Refugee Camp), "Killing Me Softly"
Best New Artist	Alanis Morissette, "Ironic"
Breakthrough Video	Smashing Pumpkins, "Tonight, Tonight"
Viewer's Choice	Bush, "Glycerine"

KURT LODER Dr. Dre arrived to do our preshow. It was the height of the East Coast/West Coast rap confrontation. He looks around, and sees Suge Knight and Tupac, and a whole bunch of people from the West Coast have showed up. There's also an East Coast contingent of West Coast sympathizers sitting around. He came to the Video Music Awards, only did our preshow, got on a plane, and left immediately. He was just so upset. And who could blame him, really? Given what happened to those guys.

ANDY SCHUON, music programming executive KISS was on tour, and we decided that it would be great to have them blow up the New York harbor with all their pyro. I was on the phone with them and they were getting ready to play in Castle Donington, the big rock festival in England. They were very close, but they wouldn't commit to it, and their manager wanted me to come over and meet with them about it. It was like four o'clock in the afternoon here in New York, so I put the phone down and literally went straight to the airport—no baggage or anything. Just get on a plane with Alex Coletti, who was going to produce the segment. Flew all night, drove all day, got to this castle. They made us get into the KISS chopper.

Imagine me dressed in khaki pants with four guys in total KISS makeup, flying over the English countryside.

So we went to the concert, through the whole show, all the way back to the castle, the next morning, we still haven't had the meeting about them coming to the Video Music Awards. Finally the next morning we have the meeting. And we're explaining that we wanted to have this giant, multi-hundred-thousand-dollar finale in total KISS spirit.

They have their heart set on doing the finale from the Statue of Liberty. And we were trying to explain we had all these rendering and drawings and things,

that if they played on the Statue of Liberty, the scale of the statue versus the band would never work, and you could never really shoot it on television. They had their heart set on it, and we were going to go back empty-handed.

And then, one of the guys in the KISS camp, said, "I've got it. Why don't we blow up the Statue of Liberty as a finale." Gene Simmons paused for what seemed like ten seconds and he turned and he said, "I don't know if we want to make that statement." Which is great, as opposed to just discounting it, and ultimately they agreed to do it on the harbor.

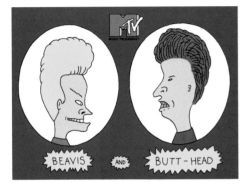

March 8, 1993–December 25, 1999

ABBY TERKUHLE, animation executive Mike Judge created Beavis while baby-sitting his kids at home.

JOHN PAYSON, producer It was one of a bunch of tapes that we were looking at for possible inclusion in *Liquid Television* and we came across "Frog Baseball," which I think is the first short that Mike did, and I just thought it was the funniest damn thing I ever saw.

DAVID FELTON, editorial executive Mike and I wrote the pilot, which was just a ten-minute thing that they showed to focus groups and it included a couple of videos. I remember the Sinéad O'Connor video where it's just her head and they say, "Wouldn't it be cool to get naked and sit on her head." What was really sort of scary was that male members of the focus groups, who were about twelve and thirteen, immediately started laughing like Beavis and Butt-head. The women, by and large, were outraged. One woman said, "God forbid a child should ever see this." So we knew we had something, but nobody knew it was going to be as big as it turned out to be.

ABBY TERKUHLE I remember going up to Mike when we got a pickup on the show and saying, "Mike, guess what? We got money to do sixty-five episodes." He turned white as a ghost, his mouth fell open, and he said, "I can't do sixty-five episodes." So I said, "Don't worry, I'll get help." He said, "I guess that means I'm gonna have to quit my band."

LARS ULRICH Some of the highlights were the really early episodes where they were dissecting the frogs and "Fire! Fire! Fire!" Beavis and Butt-head were on for six months to a year before people figured out this stuff was really insane. It sort of just snuck in there.

ABBY TERKUHLE Mike and I and a few of the MTV guys went to see Anthrax one night. We were standing around and this guy comes up to Mike and says, "Hi, I'm Joe from Grim Reaper." Mike started backing up immediately because Grim Reaper was one of the bands that Beavis and Butt-head tore apart within a show. Mike backed up, waiting for fists to fly and the guy said, "Oh man, if you had liked our video, I would've lost all respect for you and the show." Then he said, "Wait till you see our next video. It really really sucks."

Ananda Lewis

1997–present

ANANDA LEWIS I got caught outside. Our schedules are weird. We come and go as we need to. And I leave stuff at home a lot. I used to live kind of close to work. So I could leave something and forget it and run home. But I would forget that when you run outside, there are two thousand people outside that have been waiting for you all day. It's a new thing for me. So I want to fight to hold on to whatever anonymity I might have or sense of reality, like buying my own groceries. I went outside, forgetting. I was running to jump in a cab. I was like, me in New York. All of a sudden I heard my name being yelled from like thirty different voices and it really hit me where I was. It was the first time. I'm in the middle of Times Square and we got a live show going on that's pulling these kids down here by the hordes. And I'm out here, probably dressed in sweats and a T-shirt and I don't bling-bling and glam out for my own benefit. It was like a tidal wave coming at me and all I saw was people coming at me. And there was no one with me.

GEORGE MCTEAGUE, producer She likes to throw up on shoots that I'm on. We did this menu shoot for the VMAs—basically you'd just ride around on a flatbed truck for a couple of hours and see the sights of the city and she'd be talking as we were moving. We kind of had a little motion sickness that day—it could've been the fumes or whatever. But she managed to throw up. That was the first time. The second time we were going up to *Snowed In at Big Bear*. And we commuted together with a couple of other people. The road to get up to Big Bear Mountain is very long and windy and slow. She managed to puke at the end of that one, too. I told her the last time we were working together, "You puke on this shoot. I'm really gonna start taking it personally."

I don't recall exactly what I expected when I left *Rolling Stone* to work at MTV, but television turned out to be a lot different from print. In conducting interviews for magazines, I'd only needed to turn up with my tape recorder and crumpled wad of notes and natter away with the subject, alone, for three or four or maybe even more hours, preferably over drinks of some sort. In television, one turns up with other people—cameramen, audio guys, lighting folk—and then often waits a good long while as they Set Things Up. This can intimidate the interview subject, who may feel outnumbered and possibly compelled to call in some dreadful publicist or label clown for company. Headaches can quickly proliferate.

I should also mention that in the world of print interviewing, no one ever cares what you turn up *wearing*. Writers—music writers especially, I'm afraid—are generally among the least nattily turned-out professional people on the planet. (I always was, anyway.) On television, however, it's felt that one's attire must reflect the fact that one is being *seen*—very often sitting next to some orchidaceously overstyled celebrity. This unfortunate fact can catapult the neophyte on-air person into the jaws of fashion disaster, as I quickly learned.

One of my first MTV shoots was a Rock 'n' Roll Hall of Fame gathering at which a number of inductees (like the late, great Roy Orbison) and other music-biz denizens were on hand to be badgered by the press. In preparation for covering this event, I was persuaded by an MTV wardrobe person (who'd theretofore spent her time togging out VJs, I imagine) to don a bright and hideous blue silk jacket with big puffy shoulders and a ridiculous little belt across the back. Sidling into the Hall of Fame function in this preposterous garment, I immediately ran into Robbie Robertson—my benefactor!—who laughed out loud.

It took a while for a basically mumbly and reclusive person like myself to get into the swing of being an on-air extrovert—popping up in the middle of concert crowds, blinded by camera lights, attempting to say something semi-coherent into a microphone while youthful fans roiled in the background, making rude gestures and bellowing unhelpful things like *"Asshole!"*

Our weekly show, *Week in Rock*, shot in a studio on Friday nights (with free margaritas whipped up by the wardrobe department) was a lot easier to deal with. Sandra Bernhard might come in to cohost (before a bright and adorable recovering metalhead named Tabitha Soren stepped into that position on a permanent basis); the Ramones might drop by to play. People we liked a lot actually wanted to be on.

We wound up traveling quite a bit, too. When Prince announced he'd be launching a world tour in Paris in 1988, we seized upon this news as the pretext for a rare deluxe road trip: we'd cover the kickoff concert and get to do our whole show from the City of Light. This involved a lot of frantic, cram-it-all-in shooting around Paris: the banks of the Seine, the Champs Elysees, all the usual postcard vistas—and also the enormous Pere Lachaise cemetery, final resting place of such long-gone luminaries as Balzac, Proust, Oscar Wilde, Edith Piaf…and the late Doors frontman Jim Morrison, who had died in Paris, purportedly of a heart attack, in the summer of 1971. Over the years, Morrison's grave had become a shrine for dope-smoking neo-hippie globe-trotters, and we wanted to shoot it. And them, of course.

We were therefore distressed to learn, upon arriving at the cemetery entrance on the Boulevard de Menilmontant, with a French camera crew and interpreter in tow, that no filming was allowed inside. The guards seemed very serious about this. But our producer, News chief Dave Sirulnick—recently hired away from the hard-news precincts of CNN—ignored their windy gesticulations. After we shuffled away out of sight, Dave quietly instructed the camera guys to break down their equipment and hide the components in some gym bags we'd brought along. This done, we had no trouble strolling back into Pere Lachaise, gawking about innocently just like the rest of the tourists tiptoeing among the tombs.

Upon locating Morrison's grave—a squalid memorial by that time, festooned with stubbed-out joints and empty wine bottles—we reassembled our equipment and set about shooting the scruffy Doors diehards who were colorfully toking up and nodding out around the site.

The rest of the trip was considerably ritzier. Prince—who had released his brilliant *Sign 'O' the Times* album just the year before—was at the peak of his game both critically and commercially. To kick off his tour, he decided to throw a spare-no-expense post-concert party on a small island in a lake in the Bois de Boulogne, the great park of Paris. Creeping along in a crush of cars on our way there, we noticed that the woods were thick with hookers, some of them disporting themselves along the roadway in outfits of an eye-catching minimalism. Some of them, in fact, actually had mattresses tucked away back among the trees. How very Prince, we thought (although clearly this wasn't his doing). Finally, we arrived at the lakeside, where a canopied launch ferried us out across the water and deposited us at a glittering little restaurant on the island. There, champagne glasses were pressed into our unresisting hands as we wandered among what seemed endless rows of banquet tables sagging under towering mounds of seriously fancy food.

Prince himself, of course, had made himself scarce—he was huddled with bodyguards in a small, off-limits room far from the mikes of probing TV interviewers. This was fine with me, actually. I had always admired the man's refusal to prostrate himself before the ever-clamoring media. And while I might on very rare occasions over the years actually converse with him (always off-camera), it wasn't until the year 2000 that we were finally able to persuade him to sit down for an on-camera interview (in which he proved himself to be quick and witty and even self-deprecating).

We were back in Paris in 1992 to cover Guns N' Roses filming a pay-per-view TV concert, one of the highlights of which (for me, at least) was a guest appearance by the great British Invasion guitarist Jeff Beck, who'd been flown in to play on Guns' version of his old Yardbirds showstopper, "Train Kept A-Rollin'." Unfortunately, when Beck arrived in Paris, he informed his hosts that he'd forgotten the song's classic riff, and it was left to Guns bassist Duff McKagan to take him off to a room somewhere and reacquaint him with it. Beck acquitted himself beautifully at an onstage rehearsal for the show, but as soon as he walked off, he had more bad news: his tinnitus (the hearing problem that often afflicts rock musicians after years of high-volume abuse) was acting up, and he'd have to bail out of the show. With that, he turned around and flew back to London.

I wouldn't want to give the impression that the News department spends all its time jetting around the world's glamour capitals. More often than not, we find ourselves under way to someplace like Detroit. (A fine city, don't get me wrong!) However, certain stars of the sort that we cover are pretty much guaranteed to do things we want to be on hand for in places we personally do want to visit. Madonna, for example.

I first encountered Madonna in Tokyo in 1990, when she was launching her "Blonde Ambition" world tour (the one with the cone-shaped bustiers and the "I Dream of Jeannie" hairdos). The kickoff concert was staged outdoors, and of course it poured rain—not that that deterred Maddy, who's a total trouper. But there was a hot party afterward in a huge suite back at her hotel—a room booming with dance music and thronged with people, many of them topless, sweaty men writhing around a central coffee table atop which the star herself, her upper buffness encumbered only by a bra, was flinging herself about with remarkable abandon.

We'd been summoned to this disco bacchanal to do an interview, so we settled down to wait. All encounters with Madonna involve long stretches of waiting—not that we ever mind! We've waited for her in Budapest, in the Spanish mountain town of Ronda, even out in the middle of the Mojave Desert, when she was shooting her "Frozen" video. And we always utilize the generous amounts of downtime until she finally appears to set up our shot—lighting the area in which she'll be sitting just right, angling the camera just so. And then she finally arrives and marches right past the producer and over to the cameraman, takes one look at the shot he's just spent hours setting up, and announces it's all wrong.

One understands her perfectionism in this regard. Videotape, after all, like film, is forever. Or, as Maddy herself once put it: "I'm the one that has to look at this stuff for the next fifteen fuckin' years."

Meanwhile, back in the States, where most MTV News assignments actually tend to occur, we were putting in a lot of time on the rap beat. My first foray into this world was in 1988, in South-Central Los Angeles, ground zero of the burgeoning gangsta-rap phenomenon. The homicidal rivalry between the two main L.A. street gangs—the Crips and the Bloods—was the subject of an electrifying movie that year, directed by Dennis Hopper, called *Colors*. Although the film was rather awkwardly focused on the relationship between two white gang-squad cops, its soundtrack was filled with dark and hallucinatory rap music. And since the great title track was by a rapper we knew—Ice T—we approached him to give us a guided South-Central tour for *Week in Rock*.

Ice T—a smart, funny, and, of course, very streetwise guy—had grown up in South-Central, and had once been a gangbanger (as we say on the street) himself. He'd released his debut album in 1987, and by the time we met up with him for our little TV tour, he'd started having hits and living in a somewhat large way. Ice not only had the only low-rider BMW I've ever seen, but also a girlfriend, named Darlene, who was a woman of such breathtaking pulchritude that grown men could be seen to break down and weep as she twitched past them in the street. (Her boyfriend, no fool, featured her on his album covers.)

Anyway, Ice took us around to scope out the South-Central scene, pausing occasionally to offer a line of amiable jive and a kind of "Look, I'm not packing" shrug of the arms whenever a player-filled car would slow down to check us out. Failure to observe this local protocol, he explained, could possibly prompt the driver to circle the block and come squealing back around in full drive-by mode. As lifelong white people, we were goggle-eyed at this information.

Week in Rock was back in L.A. the following year to spend some time with the members of N.W.A., a group that pretty much defined the term "street credibility." Started in the L.A. exurb of Compton by Eric Wright, a drug dealer with upwardly mobile ambitions, N.W.A. ("Niggaz With Attitude") had just released the ferocious gangsta-rap classic *Straight Outta Compton*, one track on which—the notorious "Fuck tha Police"—attracted the disapproving attention of the FBI, which sent a warning letter to the group's record company and later dogged their tour, too. Since *Week in Rock* covered rap music in considerable depth, we were able to persuade one member of N.W.A.—the surprisingly cordial Ice Cube—to take us out for a cruise around Compton in his truck. Later, we went back to Cube's parents' house, where he still lived, and where the rest of the group (including the already brilliant producer Dr. Dre) eventually drifted in for an interview.

I guess I was expecting Compton to be a bombed-out Beirut of a place, but the streets were lined with small, tidy houses with neat little lawns out front. However, as Ice Cube mentioned at one point, when the sun went down, you might start hearing the sound of gunfire from the next street over, or a few streets away. Having wrapped up our interview, we didn't stick around for the demonstration.

—KURT LODER

Serena Altschul

1996–present

CHRIS CONNELLY From the start, she had this ability on air to be totally contemporary and yet not frivolous at the same time. We're both from the Upper East Side, so it was like, "Hey, someone else from the old neighborhood." Then you'd go on a shoot, and everyone would be disappointed it was you and not her. I remember guys talking directly into the camera, just to say "hi" to her!

SERENA ALTSCHUL I'm brand new, it's my first year at MTV, and they send me to *Spring Break*. Not that I wouldn't do this again, but there was this reverse bungee-jumping thing where they got me and John in it. John was like, "Yeah, sure, why not?" And so I was like, "Yeah, sure, why not?" Okay. Do we normally do this kind of stuff? I thought I was a reporter or something. And so they get us in this chair and these people who were running this facility are really strange. They're quoting biblical passages, but when you're running a reverse bungee-jumping adventure ride, you just don't want any association with death or God. And on the bottom of it, it said "Leviticus 13:4." That was scary, but back to the G force of the whole thing. They told us beforehand that it simulates a rocket launch to something in the area of three and a half G's, which I really didn't understand until about a quarter of a millisecond up in the air. And just then your lunch is in your mouth and your stomach is upside down. It's totally disgusting.

VMA 1998

DATE September 10
LOCATION Universal Amphitheater. Los Angeles
HOST Ben Stiller

JOHN NORRIS Any reaction to the nominees or…

COURTNEY LOVE I didn't really look. John. I noticed that you guys nominated Garbage a whole lot and then you didn't play the video. What is that? Garbage is like only one of the best…she's one of the only good rock stars that exists in the world. You guys piss me off.

PERFORMERS
Madonna "Shanti"/"Ray of Light"
Pras featuring "Gone Till November"/
Ol' Dirty Bastard. Mya. "Ghetto Supastar (That Is
and Wyclef Jean What You Are)"

Hole	"Celebrity Skin"
Master P	"Make 'Em Say Uhh"
Backstreet Boys	"Everybody (Backstreet's Back)"
Beastie Boys	"Intergalactic"
Brandy and Monica	"The Boy Is Mine"
Dave Matthews Band	"Stay (Wasting Time)"
Marilyn Manson	"The Dope Show"
Brian Setzer Orchestra	"Jump Jive an' Wail"

WINNERS

Best Video	Madonna. "Ray of Light"
Best Male Video	Will Smith. "Just the Two of Us"
Best Female Video	Madonna. "Ray of Light"
Best Group Video	Backstreet Boys. "Everybody (Backstreet's Back)"
Best Rap Video	Will Smith. "Gettin' Jiggy Wit It"
Best Dance Video	Prodigy. "Smack My Bitch Up"
Best Rock Video	Aerosmith. "Pink"
Best Alternative Music Video	Green Day. "Time of Your Life (Good Riddance)"
Best New Artist in a Video	Natalie Imbruglia. "Torn"
Best R&B Video	Wyclef Jean featuring Refugee Allstars. "Gone Till November"
Breakthrough Video	Prodigy. "Smack My Bitch Up"
Viewer's Choice	Puff Daddy and the Family featuring the Lox. Lil' Kim. Notorious B.I.G.. and Fuzzbubble. "It's All About the Benjamins (Rock Remix)"
Video Vanguard	Beastie Boys

MARILYN MANSON The cameramen were very specifically avoiding me below the waist when we played "The Dope Show." I felt a lot like Elvis on that night because they were real scared to show me and the transsexual woman we had dancing onstage.

ROB THOMAS His performance of "The Dope Show" was dope! That was pretty sick.

MICHELE DIX The biggest secret we had planned on the show was bringing Mariah Carey and Whitney Houston together for the top of the show, first award.

ELLI COLA They had just done the *Prince of Egypt* song and we came up with the idea that they both come out in the exact same dresses. And they both were supposed to walk on from opposite sides of the stage.

MICHELE DIX It was forty-five minutes before the show was to start live at five. Everything seemed to be moving along. I turned to Whitney's representatives and said, "She does have the dress, right?" They're like, "Of course we have the dress." They just needed to get it steamed. No problem. Then I turn and I find the person that's working with Mariah Carey. She's panic-stricken. *There is no dress.*

ART ARIANIS At about quarter to five, I go by Whitney's dressing room, after this big mix-up with the size of her dressing room. Like, Mariah's

dressing room was slightly bigger than Whitney's and so there was this big conflict and we had to solve this. Now we had a wardrobe crisis on our hands. I go by Whitney's dressing room and they hand me this wadded-up brown ball of Vera Wang fabric and it's my job now to be the wardrobe guy on the show and go and get this thing fixed for Whitney. I could not find our wardrobe guy. I grabbed a PA, said, "Find me a steamer," and this nineteen-year-old kid steamed the dress and went running back to the dressing room with it.

ELLI COLA Meanwhile, Mariah was very calm. First she's like, "What do you mean? Who didn't put the dress in the car that I was in?" But then she was just like, "Okay, we have to come up with something else." She was like, "I gotta talk to Whitney, we gotta come up with another creative idea." I'm like, "No, you don't understand. We have ten minutes until live TV, we have got to get that dress, we have got to get that dress." Whitney's on the other side going, "Why aren't we walking out yet?"

ART ARIANIS Meanwhile Mariah's dress is getting a personal police escort down a private lane and up some backroad at Universal. By five minutes to five, both women have dresses in possession. But now neither one would come out of her dressing room until the other one came out of *her* dressing room.

ELLI COLA Mariah changed in less than a minute.

ART ARIANIS She came out first, then Whitney.

ELLI COLA We were zipping her up and walking to the stage at the same time and finally she gets on the stage and literally plays with her hair for a second and they introduce her onstage.

ART ARIANIS We thought the mission was accomplished until we looked on camera and saw that Whitney's plunging neckline wasn't covering up her breast tape.

LEWIS LARGENT I had the responsibility of making sure everything was okay with Marilyn Manson that night. We have to do the big red carpet, where everybody arrives. Out comes Marilyn Manson and behind him, his girlfriend at the time, Rose McGowan. "Wow, oh my God." I've never seen anything like that before. We've all seen the risque stuff, but it's like, "I can't believe she's doing this." Butt-naked. I was thinking, "I understand why she's doing it, but who's gonna publish this picture?" We're all watching it happen, but it's one of those things that nobody's ever gonna be able to see, unless you read *Playboy* or something. I thought she was gonna wear the dress the whole night, but what happened was she changed it and went back into this very conservative look.

Dave Holmes

1998–present

DAVE HOLMES The original plan was to go down to *Spring Break* for a couple of days and do *Say What? Karaoke* and see some other things here and there. And I was going home on March 13, my birthday is March 14, and I realized I had a couple of days in my schedule and I'm in Cancún, which is one of the most beautiful places in the world with all these beautiful people and a ton of friends from work. Hell, why don't I just stay for a couple of extra and celebrate it here with drinks and fun and music and coworkers and stuff like that. So I did. And it just happened that the wrap party for the show we did coincided with my birthday. Got to celebrate it with Jerry Springer. He showed up at the after-party, got some pictures. It

was good stuff. It was a hangover that lasted a week and an half, but it was worth it.

GEORGE MCTEAGUE, producer First time I met Dave Holmes, I actually worked on the VJ search, which basically comprised a lot of volunteers from our department to go downstairs for a full day and interview over two thousand people. So you'd sit in this little booth and interview these people who thought they could be a VJ. And then if you thought this person was good you'd give their application a little star and send them on.

None of the people I picked even got close to making it. But I had an interest in the show 'cause it was a cool idea. I worked on the day that had five

contestants, Dave among them, Jesse, and a few others. I actually floor-produced that show. I was out at Virgin Megastore where they had to run through and get their CD choices and explain why they picked what for whatever reason. So I got an idea that he was a nice guy and I actually was rooting for him the whole entire time because he seemed to know more about music than anybody else and that he was likeable.

He was a very atypical VJ. He wasn't the—no offense to Dave—he wasn't the pretty boy, but he really seemed to be genuine about music and was passionate about it. I thought he had a great personality and a great sense of humor, which I thought was cool.

Diary

JESSE IGNJATOVIC A lot of the inspiration for *Diary* is from the Bob Dylan movie *Don't Look Back*. I wanted to be like D.A. Pennebaker: just hang with this person for days and days and days. You get those moments when their guard is down. I mean...if anyone wants to know about Dylan at that time, you watch *Don't Look Back*. That's where you really get the idea of who this person is.

Kid Rock is a person who loves life. He was just great to be around because of his complete and utter appreciation for rock 'n' roll and the rock 'n' roll lifestyle and enjoying it and not overthinking it and not posing. He's just a great hang. I spent a lot of time on the tour bus with him. And you know, he's playing CDs, he's going from Lynyrd Skynyrd to old country music—like George Jones–type stuff, to hip-hop, and drinking a lot of beers. And talking on the bus. Exactly what you would think being on a rock 'n' roll bus is like. Then his preshow thing where he had to smoke, drink some booze, get wine, get psyched, and go out there and just tear it up. I mean, being around those guys, it's not work. It's total pleasure.

We finally got around to doing one with Manson. And his persona is not really how he is. I think he's a very, very cerebral, intellectual person. And a very thoughtful person. Going to Japan with him was great just to see how giving he is to his fans, and to see that he's so ultimately American, being in Japan and eating at McDonald's.

Out of all the episodes, the one with DMX is my favorite. I was nervous. I didn't know what to expect. From the get-go, he treated me incredibly well and was very generous. He also had this incredible aura and intensity about him. So many artists try to say that they live in the moment, that every minute could be dangerous. He *is* that. He lives life completely on gut instinct. From the way he eats, to the way he drives, to the way he picks and chooses who he's gonna talk to and what he's gonna say. When you're shooting him and looking through the eyepiece, you know that every frame of that footage is important. I walked away from that first shoot with him down in Florida just completely blown away by this guy. There's so many different people in DMX. He just changes constantly so you never know what you're gonna get.

Before I went down there, people said, "Just don't drive with him!" His reputation as a driver precedes him. When I first got there, I walked in with my camera and we were introduced. He says, "Wanna go for a ride?" And I was like, "Sure! Can I shoot?" He goes, "You can shoot anything you want." So we got in the car and he just drove and took me to an area called Little Haiti. It's a very poor area way outside the whole Miami Beach area where there's a lot of people who emigrated from Haiti. And he was driving around there with me blasting "Superfly" by Curtis Mayfield over and over at, like, eleven, just driving around, saying hi to the neighborhood kids. And yeah, he drives fast. He drives angry. When he's on a street or an avenue, he believes that there's a way for him to be in the lead somewhere down the line. Like three traffic lights ahead, he'll be in the lead of everyone, which never happens, 'cuz there's always gonna be a car in front of you. But he could literally be

at a standstill in traffic and still try to find a way to move ahead of a car.

Then there was the West Side Highway experience, when we were shooting in Yonkers all day for the last part of the show. He had to be on *TRL* that day. And in true DMX style, he was saying to the label people: "Why are you rushing me to do this *TRL* thing when I gave my day for this? This is what I want to do. I want to show these guys what I came from, what I'm about. Now you're trying to make me cut this short and go do that." So he was sort of angry about that. And of course, he's always losing people. Our camera crew was in another van with people from the label—there ain't no chance they're gonna be with us. They're gone within two minutes of driving. So he was sort of bumming and we had to race back to *TRL*. I felt like—no disrespect to people who've been in wars—but I felt like I was in 'Nam, or something, sitting in that car while he was driving. It was so intense. Just feeling like at any moment you could die. That's what it felt like. I was shooting him and trying not to like take my left eye off the eyepiece to look out the front window to see what was coming up. 'Cuz we were traveling at well over a hundred and twenty miles an hour, weaving in and out of traffic. And I'd be watching his face sort of grimace a little when he knew it was a close pass.

I don't know if it's DMX trying to concentrate. I just think that it's like...he's just doing it. He's doing it, and he may be having a smoke at the same time. I mean, he doesn't think that way, I don't think. I just feel like he puts it all out there. And whatever happens, happens. Like, his life is totally in God's hands. There's no posing for the camera. He is who he is and you can roll with it or you can get out.

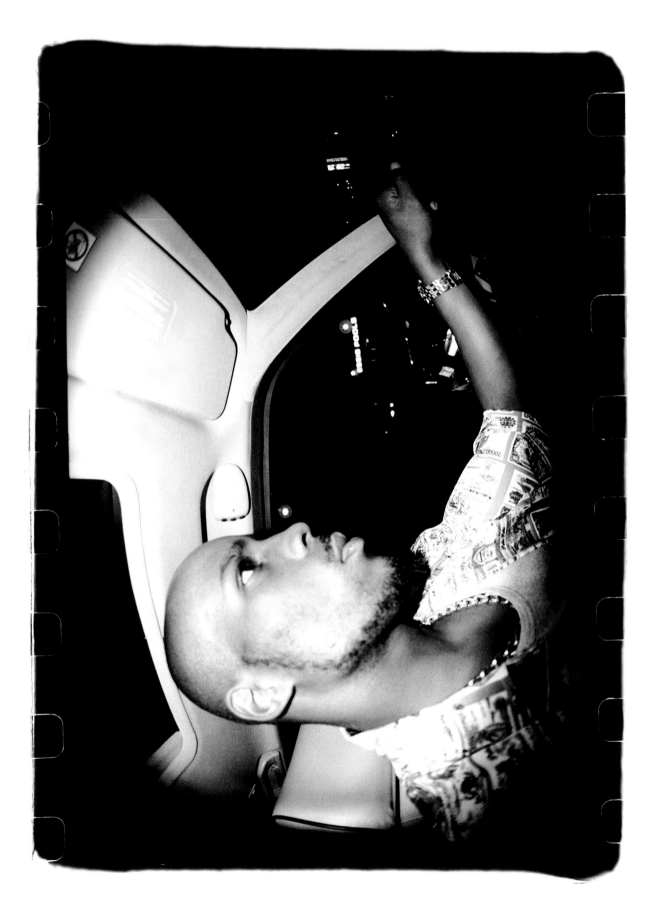

Jackass

Brian McFayden

1999–present

VMA 1984

DATE September 14
LOCATION Radio City Music Hall, New York
HOSTS Bette Midler and Dan Aykroyd

PERFORMERS

David Bowie	"Blue Jean"
Huey Lewis and the News	"I Want a New Drug"
Madonna	"Like a Virgin"
Ray Parker, Jr.	"Ghostbusters"
Rod Stewart	"Infatuation"
Tina Turner	"What's Love Got to Do with It"
ZZ Top	"Sharp Dressed Man"

WINNERS

Best Video	The Cars, "You Might Think"
Best Male Video	David Bowie, "China Girl"
Best Female Video	Cyndi Lauper, "Girls Just Want to Have Fun"
Best New Artist	Eurythmics, "Sweet Dreams"

JOE DAVOLA, former executive Madonna's record company didn't want her to do the song that she did on the show, which was "Like a Virgin." The album was just coming out that week, and they wanted to do something that was on the charts already. That was a big struggle between her and her record company. She won and did "Like a Virgin." During the rehearsal, when she was rolling all along the floor in that bustier, her breasts popped out, and that got caught on camera during the rehearsals. That tape circulated through the offices for the next couple years.

MADONNA I'll never forget the time you put that camera up my dress when I was rolling around on the floor. The first MTV awards, remember that, I didn't know what I was doing. I had no idea my dress was up, but you took advantage of it with your zoom lens, didn't you.

Madonna

CHRISTINA AGUILERA Madonna definitely opened the door for a lot of other female artists to get out there and not be afraid. As her song says, "express yourself." Be bold and courageous and reinvent yourself. She's the re-inventor; the mother of it. Hopefully I'll be able to follow in her footsteps.

MARK GOODMAN I was really excited to meet her and interview her and stuff. But who would have imagined that she would become such a cultural phenomenon? In fact I met her years later and I said, "I'm Mark Goodman. Remember me? I met you before you were Madonna." And she says, "I was always Madonna."

DAVE SIRULNICK, news and production executive Kurt and Madonna has been a decade-long, exciting sort of sparring match. Kurt loves Madonna and I think Madonna respects and really likes Kurt because she knows she's going to have a good time with him. Madonna can be an intimidating presence. Yet, Kurt handles her and deals with her probably better than anybody else.

KURT LODER She's done a lot of interviews. When she comes in with people doing television, she wants to check the lights, she wants the monitor, she wants to direct the whole thing. As she puts it, "I have to look at this fucking stuff for the next fifteen years, it better be good." So what are you going to do? She moves things around and then everybody puts them back where they were in the first place and then we start.

DAVE SIRULNICK There was one time, again back in Spain, we were doing a sit-down interview with her, and it was cold. We had some space heaters, but because we were in this old stone castle, there's only enough outlets and electrical power for camera equipment and one of the heaters. But we say we'll put three heaters around her maybe psychologically she'll think its warmer. You can't slip something like that by Madonna. She sits down, she feels one of them. "You guys are trying to fool me, these two things aren't even working. Get these things out of here."

KURT LODER We had set her up in Spain for this shoot in a monastery or something. It was for the "Take a Bow" video. We found this beautiful location. It was gorgeous. It was fabulous. Even I was dressed pretty nicely. It was one of those rare occasions. So she shows up in this really nice dress. And then decides it's too cold and takes this ratty old sweater that your grandmother wouldn't even wear, puts it around her shoulders, and wears it throughout the entire interview.

CARSON DALY When Madonna came on *TRL* I was so excited that she was booked as a guest because I was always such a big fan, but I was freaking out 'cause I thought, here's somebody that couldn't give two craps about me, obviously has no clue who I am, doesn't watch this show.

So she came on and was really down to earth. She looked me in the eye and she came out and was like, "What's up, Carson, how's it going?" No attitude, no problems. And then we're on the air and we were going into the Christina Aguilera video. This is when all the press about Christina and me was going around.

I asked Madonna, "What do you think of Christina Aguilera, she says you're a huge influence or her. Do you know about her?" Madonna makes some crack like, "Probably not as much as you do," or something. She alluded to the fact that she was privy to the teen gossip.

The Real World

SEBASTIAN BACH I find myself morbidly fascinated with *The Real World*. It's like watching a train wreck.

ROB FOX, news and docs producer MTV wanted to do a soap opera, so they hired these soap opera people. MTV's notorious for its low budgets, so when they came in with the budget for what it would actually cost to do a soap opera, MTV balked. They were like, "Oh, my God. We can't afford that, that's ridiculous. Here's the number, this is what we can afford." The soap opera people looked at it and went, "Well, if we get rid of the writers, and get rid of the actors, get rid of the set..."

MARY-ELLIS BUNIM, co-creator/executive producer The city becomes the eighth roommate; it adds a lot of character to the surroundings. I mean, New York can be quite oppressive, but it can be one of the most exciting places in the world.

JON MURRAY, co-creator/executive producer Then you look at Miami. And my God! That was sort of sexual-tension city. The tropical heat. Something about that just makes people go a little wild. And I think that came through in the Miami season.

MARY-ELLIS BUNIM And San Francisco had a unique and very strong gay culture that was interesting on the show, and that was fascinating. And London showed us how uptight Brits are.

JON MURRAY The Europeans are a little different. They're a little more cynical, a little more wary of cameras. And Seattle taught us how intolerant and cynical people can be when there are cameras around them.

MARY-ELLIS BUNIM New Orleans was a wall-to-wall party.

JON MURRAY The first night, they went down to the local drugstore. There was a crowd of about twenty young people from Tulane following them down there.

MARY-ELLIS BUNIM There was always a crowd outside that house.

New York, 1992

CAST MEMBERS Eric, Becky, Julie, Heather, Andre, Norman, and Kevin

JULIE I didn't know what the show was going to be about, but they did say, "Oh, it'll be seven people from all different parts of the country." When I got to the loft I felt kind of set up: I was the only one who didn't know New York. I think the reason the cameras followed me around so much was because I didn't know anybody else in the city. I only had the camera crew to hang out with.

JON MURRAY Our cast members can't be so sure of themselves and so set in their ways that they're not gonna be affected by their experiences.

MARY-ELLIS BUNIM If they have anything in common, it's that they're all in the process of defining themselves. That process goes on usually up to about age twenty-four, twenty-five. We try to capture that phase where people are trying on lots of different hats. And trying to define how they feel about things. Willing to explore that. It's really exciting.

Los Angeles, 1993

CAST MEMBERS Beth S., Jon, Irene, Glen, Dominic, Tami, Aaron, David, and Beth A.

MARY-ELLIS BUNIM We've had the opportunity to deal with a wide variety of really important issues. And we try to present both sides so that the audience can participate in the experience and not be hit over the head with a judgment. The second season we followed a woman as she decided to have an abortion and went through lots of exploration with her roommates, one of whom was a fundamentalist

Christian. And he had a really tough time, as you can imagine, but eventually came to realize that she was a friend of his. He wasn't approving her behavior. He really loved her. It was just an incredible lesson.

TAMI I think *The Real World* was stressful at times. It has its goods and bads. You have no private time. You're forced to interact when you don't want to. Then again, you come away with something you remember for the rest of your life.

San Francisco, 1994

CAST MEMBERS Rachel, Pam, Judd, Cory, Puck, Jo, Mohammed, and Pedro

MARY-ELLIS BUNIM Our most poignant experience on the show was the season of San Francisco and Pedro Zamora. He wrote us a letter asking to be on this show, explaining his situation and explaining his experience as an AIDS educator. We sat down with him and said, "You know, Pedro, this is possibly incredibly stressful for you and may compromise your current health." And he said, "This is my life's work. And if you can give me a forum and it reaches just a few people, I feel my work is accomplished."

JON MURRAY He also said, "If I'm not going on *The Real World*, I'm just continuing to march in front of the White House and get arrested and do all the other things I'm doing to try and bring AIDS education to people." He said his life wouldn't be stress-free no matter what he did. And also, as a young single man, he told us, "The idea of going to San Francisco and getting away from my family in Miami, my very large Cuban family, is very exciting. I don't know how long my life will be, but don't deny me the chance to live it to the fullest."

PAM Knowing Pedro changed my life in so many ways, including my relationship to medicine. Before Pedro, I'd had an academic interest in HIV/AIDS. I felt like Pedro was walking me through the disease and through death, the way a close friend might take your hand for a stroll.

MARY-ELLIS BUNIM And then he went to San Francisco and fell in love with Sean. And it was the first time we were able to capture a real romance, a real love story. And it was just was a beautiful build to the story and culminated in the ribbon ceremony.

SEAN Pedro and I were pretty open to the whole idea of putting our relationship on the air. We had no idea that they would make us such a central part of the whole thing. The crew gave us plenty of time without cameras. They were very respectful, very concerned about what they were doing. I was pretty happy about the portrayal of Pedro and our relationship.

JON MURRAY That was amazing because you also had Puck, who said, "I don't care if Pedro is a saint. I don't like the guy." And he was just so refreshingly un-PC. It was just an amazing contrast. And ultimately it was Pedro, the kid whose health was challenged, standing up to Puck while his roommates cowered.

It's been so exciting, as a gay man, to have this network so completely open its arms to what the show is about, which is the idea of diversity. Never once have we received a note saying, "We don't want to see that close-up of Pedro and Sean kissing." I mean, they really are color-blind and any other kind of blind to the way they approach any notes on the show.

PRESIDENT BILL CLINTON In his short life, Pedro educated and enlightened our nation. He taught all of us that AIDS is a disease with a human face and one that affects every American, indeed, every citizen of the world. And he taught people living with AIDS how to fight for their rights and live with dignity.

MARY-ELLIS BUNIM Things were decidedly dull. And Neil was a Ph.D. from Oxford who had a fascination with punk rock. So his alter ego at night would don the dark makeup. I don't know what kind of music it was, but the most bizarre and obscene lyrics would come out of his mouth. He was out performing one night and there was a guy in the audience heckling him. He provoked Neil to jump off the stage, and then Neil French-kissed him. The guy almost bit his tongue off. They rushed Neil to the hospital and sewed his tongue back in his mouth. Our most articulate cast member couldn't speak for six weeks. He had to communicate with us via his computer, which had a voice synthesizer. He was so irritated that the synthesizer sounded like an American.

SHARON Neil's got a very unique sense of humor. It's very English. He just likes to shock and loves to provoke and get a rise out of people. He's very prickly, thorny. But he's such a soft, mild, gentle guy.

JON MURRAY I can remember an interview where he's saying, "I thought having my tongue ripped out of my mouth was the worst thing that could happen.

good Cuban girl. Had a boyfriend. And Flora was just dying to know what was going on in that room. So Dan was lifting her up and trying to squeeze her through the bathroom window. And the window broke and went crashing down. It was a great moment.

MARY-ELLIS BUNIM They never really did find out what was happening in that shower. And neither did we.

MELISSA We were a bunch of horny, crazy people having a good time in a big house.

Boston, 1997

CAST MEMBERS Syrus, Elka, Montana, Kameelah, Genesis, Sean, and Jason

KAMEELAH Being on *The Real World* was like being a part of history, at least a part of our generation's history. Someone who grew up in the '60s might say, "I went to Woodstock." Now I can say, "I was on *The Real World*." It was the best experience I've ever had. A chance to leave my normal environment. To put

London, 1995

CAST MEMBERS Jay, Kat, Jacinda, Mike, Sharon, Lars, and Neil

MARY-ELLIS BUNIM The famous London story is about Neil. I mean, we had a hard time with the London season because our American kids weren't permitted to work in England. And so, while we had Jacinda going out to model, and that was interesting, we had Mike and Jay playing pool and occasionally Rollerblading in the park.

JON MURRAY And watching satellite American television at three in the morning, desperate for American culture.

But the worst thing is speaking with an American accent."

Miami, 1996

CAST MEMBERS Dan, Sarah, Flora, Melissa, Cynthia, Joe, and Mike

JON MURRAY One of our most popular shows was when Melissa, Mike, and a waitress he met ended up in the hot tub together. And clothes started to come off. And then they all went into the shower in the upstairs boys' room. And Flora and Dan were trying to see what was going on in there. Melissa was this

myself in a pressure cooker and see how I would respond.

Seattle, 1998

CAST MEMBERS Janet, David, Nathan, Rebecca, Stephen, Lindsay, and Irene

DAVID *The Real World* was seriously a good experience for me, even with its dark side. I grew a lot. I made some great friends. The most profound effect it had on my life was it took away my anonymity.

Honolulu, 1999

CAST MEMBERS Teck, Amaya, Colin, Ruthie, Matt, Kaia, and Justin

MARY-ELLIS BUNIM The second night, Ruthie had alcohol poisoning and passed out. And her roommates had to save her, drag her into the shower. They finally called 911, got an ambulance, and had her stomach pumped.

RUTHIE I let alcohol take over my life. I didn't do it on purpose; it's just something that happened.

KAIA We went into our season with a bang. Alcohol poisoning on the second day? It wasn't exactly easy to bounce back.

JON BUNIM What was really interesting about that was she continued to do some things when she was using too much alcohol. A couple of her roommates turned to us during their weekly interview, saying, "Hey, can you guys do something about this?" We said, "No, you guys are roommates and you have to figure this out." And finally they basically did an intervention with her and told her that this behavior was gonna get her killed one day, that if she wanted to be a part of this house she had to go into rehab. Then they would welcome her back after she finished it. It was amazing to see a group of young people take the responsibility to deal with their roommate. And you know, it wasn't just a TV show. It was about dealing with another human being they cared about. And I think that was a really important show for our audience, many of whom are on college campuses where alcohol is being abused. And the fact that they stepped up to the plate and dealt with it, I think, was incredibly courageous on their part.

RUTHIE God, what an idiot I was. What can I say? You live, you learn, you move on. I strive to be so positive. I want people to know that there are many different sides of me. There's so much more to me than drinking.

MARY-ELLIS BUNIM Our rule of thumb is, we don't step in unless somebody is on the verge of seriously harming himself or someone else.

New Orleans, 2000

CAST MEMBERS Melissa, Danny, Julie, Jamie, Kelley, Matt, and David

MELISSA As a viewer, I used to wonder how anyone could bitch while living in a mansion. Now I realize that though we have a mansion with really cool rugs and furniture, we don't have a job to which we're committed; we don't have obligations. What we have is way too much time to think. And that's where the drama starts.

New York, 2001

CAST MEMBERS Lori, Mike, Rachael, Malik, Coral, Kevin, and Nicole

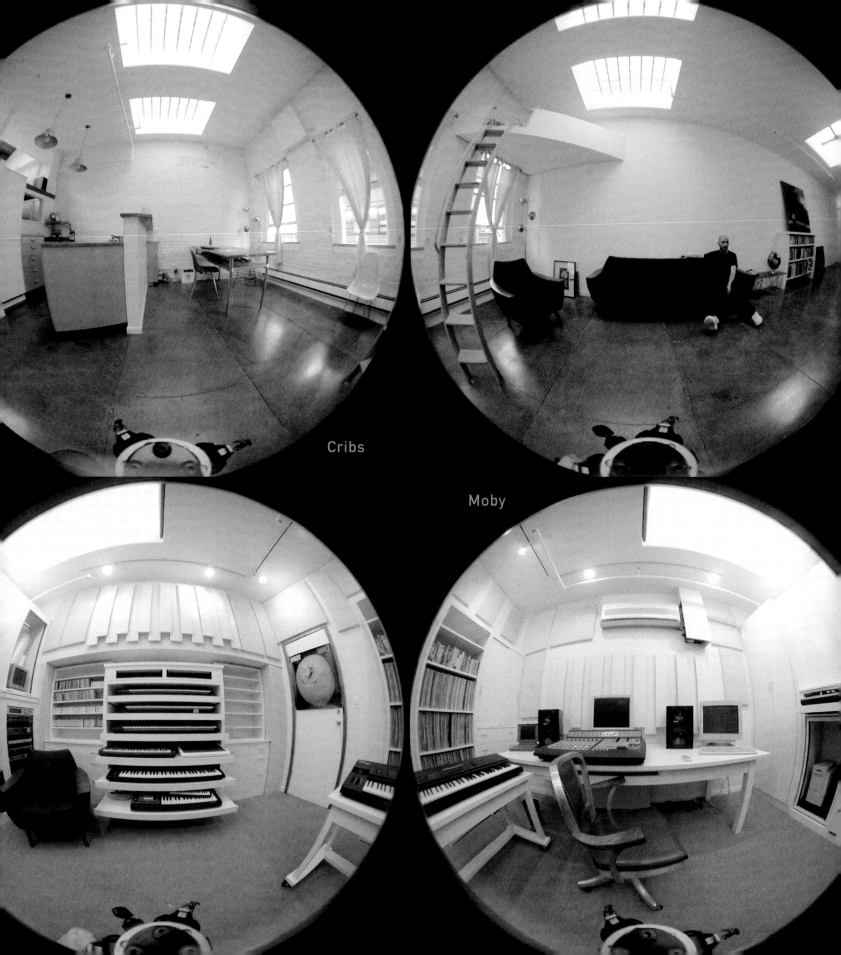

Cribs

Moby

Daria

Aeon Flux

The Maxx

DISTINGUISHING CHARACTERISTIC Teen brainiac
SPIN-OFF FROM *Beavis and Butt-head*
NICKNAME ACCORDING TO BEAVIS AND BUTT-HEAD Diarrhea
Age 16 when show began in 1997

TRACY GRANDSTAFF, writer/voice of Daria MTV didn't have a huge budget for *Daria*. It was a one-off. No one knew if it was going to be popular. They had the writers do the voices of a lot of the characters. And they threw me into the booth. One of the voices I ended up doing was Daria.

JANEANE GAROFALO *Daria*? I have only seen a handful. Many people think I do the voice of Daria which is actually not true. I'm flattered by that, I guess.

TRACY GRANDSTAFF I give her full credit. She can take it. I'm the poor man's Janeane. In fact, she was saying on another channel that people in the East Village scream at her, "Yo Daria, you suck."

Great, she can take that credit. I don't need that.

Celebrity Deathmatch

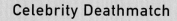

ABBY TERKUHLE, animation executive I think people want to be in the show, it's sort of a rite of passage. Eric Fogel and John Lin got a dozen roses from Whoopi Goldberg and the card read, "I love you guys, I love what you do, and I love that I won." She was in a Comic Relief fight where she kicked Robin Williams's and Billy Crystal's ass so she really loved it. I think maybe early on Kathie Lee Gifford said some disparaging remark about the show. She didn't like her portrayal. I recall Jennifer Lopez not liking the voice. She felt that we didn't capture her voice properly. She had no response about the way she was depicted visually in the show, which is quite outrageous. She had this butt that was quite over the top. Had no problem with that. Apparently she didn't like the way she sounded.

off." And I listened to it and said maybe I can. So I spent the next four days really really trying to memorize it. That's all I did. I mean, it's random. Maybe there's a story to it but I didn't quite get it. And it was really difficult and I had cue cards and I really screwed it up.

CARSON DALY There was a guy dressed up like a gorilla holding Gwen Stefani's cue cards in the back, because the song, if you've ever done karaoke, is like the hardest song in the world to do. The lyrics are going by so fast. He was throwing these cue cards and she was trying to read it. They were upside down and it was real funny.

It's the End of the World As We Know It

DATE December 31, 1999
LOCATION Times Square
PERFORMERS Goo Goo Dolls, Blink-182, 98 Degrees, Christina Aguilera, Jay-Z, Bush, and Puff Daddy
DJS DJ Skribble, Funk Master Flex, Mark Ronson and Freestylers

JOHN NORRIS There had been a lot of talk about potential problems, all kinds of rumors. There was a popular one about stacks of body bags being stored in an abandoned building here in Manhattan because they "know" something's going to go off, something's going to happen. This didn't exactly settle your nerves too much.

And then all the manhole covers being welded and all the checks of all the trash cans around Times Square . . . I worried to the point where I said, "Okay, I'll do the outside location, I'll do the platform," which is where they always want to put me, by the way. I'll do the outside platform but I don't want to be there at midnight. 'Cause I thought if there were any incidents, they were going to happen around midnight.

But then you started to worry less when you saw that midnight was going off in an amazing way and without a hitch in time zone after time zone around the world.

CHRIS CONNELLY So we're counting down and all the rest of it and I'm out there with Jessica Simpson and Nick Lachey. And they're having a great time and Jessica Simpson had this really tumultuous year, you know. Not only had she become a star but she'd been in the hospital a bunch of times with a kidney

ailment, so she's glad just to be standing in twenty-degree weather. And Nick is in love with her and all the rest of it. So you know ten, nine, eight and the thing goes off and I just remember noise and sound and I turn around and they are *inhaling* each other.

TOM DELONGE I remember mostly the artists that were there were hitting on me the whole entire night, like . . .

MARK HOPPUS Gavin Rossdale.

TOM DELONGE Yeah, he was. Apparently he just thinks we're super-cute.

MARK HOPPUS Tom thinks people's idea of hitting on him is saying, "Hey, how's it going."

GWEN STEFANI I remember I was in London and they called me up and asked me if I wanted to do that song. I said, "Let me listen to it and see if I can pull it

Super Bowl XXXV

NELLY My manager called me and asked me if I wanted to be a part of the halftime show and I was like: "Hell, yeah."

ALEX COLETTI, executive producer We decided to do a battle of the bands, a battle of pop and rock. And the minute we started talking about it Aerosmith seemed to be the obvious choice. And *NSYNC did, as well. I guess when I initially pitched it I was coming off the football: two teams collide. It was what the Super Bowl is about. But—and I think wisely so—Aerosmith decided to go in the opposite direction: "Let's let it be pop *meets* rock. Let's let it be pop plus rock equals better."

BETH MCCARTHY MILLER I think everybody was a little nervous before the first day of rehearsal. On paper, it's like, "Aerosmith and *NSYNC. Okay. I get the pop and rock thing. But, God! Aerosmith and *NSYNC?"

NELLY When I came through the door in the first rehearsal they were already going through a few steps. To meet Steve, and Joe, all of Aerosmith and *NSYNC… Not like I'm a crazed fan, but I definitely appreciate what they do musically. I'm a real big Mary J fan. So that was real hot to see her. I didn't see Britney until we rehearsed out on the field, but she was cool peoples too, it was great.

BRITNEY SPEARS I hadn't met Steven Tyler yet—so our first meeting was onstage at rehearsal. I was overwhelmed with excitement and felt that led to a great rehearsal. I mean the group is a legend. I've always loved Aerosmith's music and it was great to be a part of the rock world.

ALEX COLETTI I'm standing up on stage with Joe Perry while he's playing the guitar and he goes, "This is really fucking cool." And to just see someone like Joe Perry who's played stadiums around the world. With these guys it's hard to impress them. Who've done the Oscars, the Grammys, and Joe Perry's looking at me going, "This is pretty cool. I'm playing the Super Bowl." I'm like, "You think that's cool. I'm hanging out with Joe Perry! At the Super Bowl!"

BRITNEY SPEARS I've watched the Super Bowl halftime show since I was a kid so it was really cool to be an actual part of it.

NELLY My manager said it's with Aerosmith and *NSYNC and Britney Spears and Mary J and I told him, "I don't give a damn who it's with." I was Super Bowl struck. It wasn't the star factor. To me, the Super Bowl is bigger than any star. That's the biggest thing we've ever done, will probably be the biggest thing we ever do, unless we do it again. 'Cuz that's the biggest audience ever. Ain't no toppin' that.

When I was
watching MTV
growing up
in the mid '80's
it influenced me
to make music
because I thought,
this sucks.
I bet
there is a kid
right now
who's thinking
the same thing
and will come up
in a few years
and change music
because of what
he is seeing
now on
MTV.

—BILLY CORGAN